NATIONAL QUALIFICATIONS

General & Foundation ENGLISH

The National Qualifications Examination Paper and the Scottish Certificate of Education Examination Papers are reprinted by special permission of THE SCOTTISH QUALIFICATIONS AUTHORITY

ISBN 0 7169 9330 9

ROBERT GIBSON · Publisher
17 Fitzroy Place, Glasgow, G3 7SF.

CONTENTS

1996 Foundation Level — Reading 3
1997 Foundation Level — Reading 9
1998 Foundation Level — Reading 17
1999 Foundation Level — Reading 27
2000 Foundation Level — Reading 35
1994 General Level — Reading 42
1995 General Level — Reading 49
1996 General Level — Reading 56
1997 General Level — Reading 63
1998 General Level — Reading 69
2000 General Level — Reading 78
2000 Foundation, General and Credit Levels — Writing 85

1996
TUESDAY, 7 MAY
10.50 AM – 11.40 AM

ENGLISH
STANDARD GRADE
Foundation Level
Reading
Text

Read carefully the passage. It will help if you read it twice. When you have done so, answer the questions. Use the spaces provided in the Question/Answer booklet.

THE BEAR

1 The bear had been a real danger, though at the time they had all laughed. No, Mama had never laughed, but Lyddie and Charles and the babies had laughed until their bellies ached. Lyddie still thought of them as the babies. She probably always would. Agnes had been four and Rachel six that November of 1843—the year of the bear.

2 It had been Charles's fault, if fault there was. He had fetched in wood from the shed and left the door ajar. But the door had not shut tight for some time, so perhaps he'd shut it as best he could. Who knows?

3 At any rate, Lyddie looked up from the pot of oatmeal she was stirring over the fire, and there in the doorway was a massive black head, the nose up and smelling, the tiny eyes bright with hunger.

4 "Don't nobody yell," she said softly. "Just back up slow and quiet to the ladder and climb up to the loft. Charlie, you get Agnes, and Mama, you take Rachel." She heard her mother whimper. "Shhh," she continued, her voice absolutely even. "It's all right long as nobody gets upset. Just take it nice and gentle, ey? I'm watching him all the way, and I'll yank the ladder up after me."

5 They obeyed her, even Mama, though Lyddie could hear her sucking in her breath. Behind Lyddie's back, the ladder creaked, as two by two, first Charles and Agnes, then Mama and Rachel, climbed up into the loft. Lyddie glared straight into the bear's eyes, daring him to step forward into the cabin. Then when the ladder was silent and she could hear the slight rustling above her as the family settled themselves on the straw mattresses, she backed up to the ladder and, never taking her eyes off the bear, inched her way up to the loft. At the top she almost fell backward onto the platform. Charles dragged her onto the mattress beside her mother.

6 The racket released the bear from the charm Lyddie seemed to have placed on him. He banged the door aside and rushed in toward the ladder, but Charles snatched it. The bottom rungs swung out, hitting the beast in the nose. The blow startled him for a moment, giving Lyddie a chance to help Charles haul the ladder up onto the platform and out of reach. The old bear roared in frustration and waved at the empty air with his huge paws, then reared up on his hind legs. He was so tall that his nose nearly touched the edge of the loft. The little girls cried out. Their mother screamed, "Oh Lord, deliver us!"

7 "Hush," Lyddie commanded. "You'll just make him madder." The cries were swallowed up in anxious gasps of breath. Charles's arms went around the little ones, and Lyddie put a firm grip on her mother's shoulder. It was trembling, so Lyddie relaxed her fingers and began to stroke. "It's all right," she murmured. "He can't reach us." But could he climb the supports? It didn't seem likely. Could he take a mighty leap and . . ? No, she tried to breathe deeply and evenly and keep her eyes fixed on those of the beast. He fell to all fours and, tossing his head, broke off from her gaze as though embarrassed.

8 He began to explore the cabin. He was hungry, obviously, and looking for the source of the smell that had drawn him in. He knocked over the churning jug and licked at it, but Lyddie had cleaned it too well that morning and the bear soon gave up trying. Before he found the great pot of oatmeal hanging over the fire, he had turned over the table and the benches and upended the spinning wheel. Lyddie held her breath, praying that he wouldn't break anything. Charles and she would try to mend things but he was only ten and she thirteen. They hadn't their father's skill or experience and they couldn't afford to replace any of the household goods.

9 Next the beast knocked over a jar of butter. He smacked it across the floor where it hit the overturned bench, but did not shatter.

10 At last he came to the oatmeal, bubbling over the fire. He thrust his head deep into the pot and howled with pain as his nose met the boiling porridge. He threw back his head, but in doing so jerked the pot off the hook, and when he turned, he was wearing it over his head like a black pumpkin. The bear was too stunned, it seemed, simply to lower his neck and let the pot fall off. He danced about the room in pain on four, then two legs, the pot covering his head, the boiling oatmeal raining down his thick neck and coat.

11 He knocked about, searching for the way out, but when he found the open door, managed to push it shut. Battering the door with his pot-covered head, he tore it off its leather hinges and loped out into the dark. For a long time they could hear him crashing through the bush until, at last, the quiet November night gathered about them once more.

12 Then they began to laugh. Rachel first, throwing back her dark curls and showing the spaces where her pretty little teeth had been only last summer. Then Agnes joined in with her shrill four-year-old shout, and next Charles's not yet manly giggle.

13 "Whew," Lyddie said. "Lucky I'm so ugly. A pretty girl couldn't a scared that old rascal!"

14 "You ain't ugly!" Rachel cried. But they laughed louder than ever, Lyddie the loudest of all, until the tears of laughter and relief ran down her thin cheeks, and her belly cramped and doubled over. When had she laughed so much? She could not remember.

Adapted from *Lyddie* by Katherine Paterson

[*END OF PASSAGE*]

Marks

QUESTIONS

Write your answers in the spaces provided.

Look at Paragraphs 1 to 3.

1. **Write down** an expression which shows that the children laughed a lot about the bear.

   ______________________________ 2 ■ 0

2. (*a*) Why might it be Charles's fault that the bear gets into the cabin?

   ______________________________ 2 ■ 0

   (*b*) Why might it not be Charles's fault?

   ______________________________ 2 ■ 0

3. What is Lyddie doing when the bear appears?

   ______________________________ 2 ■ 0

4. **Write down three** things about the bear which Lyddie notices. 2 1 0

   (i) ______________________________

   (ii) ______________________________

   (iii) ______________________________

Look at Paragraph 4.

5. Complete the following sentences about Lyddie's instructions to the family.

   (i) Everyone is to be __________ and move __________ . 2 1 0

   (ii) They are to climb the __________ up to the __________ . 2 1 0

   (iii) Mama is to take __________ and Charles is to take __________ . 2 1 0

Marks

6. How can you tell that the mother is afraid?

____ 2 ■ 0

7. Write down an expression which shows that Lyddie gives the instructions **very** calmly.

____ 2 1 0

Look at Paragraphs 5 and 6.

8. How does Lyddie try to keep the bear's attention away from the family?

____ 2 ■ 0

9. Which **two** things tell Lyddie that the family is up in the loft? 2 1 0

(i) ____

(ii) ____

10. Write down one word which shows that Lyddie climbs the ladder slowly.

[ ] 2 ■ 0

11. Explain fully how Lyddie and Charles get the chance to pull up the ladder.

____

____ 2 1 0

Look at Paragraph 7.

12. "'It's all right,' she murmured. 'He can't reach us.'"

What **two** thoughts does Lyddie have which show she is not as confident as she sounds? 2 1 0

(i) ____

(ii) ____

Marks

Look at Paragraphs 8 and 9.

13. Give **two** reasons why Lyddie prays that the bear won't break anything. **2 1 0**

(i) ______________________________

(ii) ______________________________

14. Write down three things the bear disturbs as he explores the cabin. **2 1 0**

(i) ______________________________

(ii) ______________________________

(iii) ______________________________

Look at Paragraph 10.

15. Why does the bear howl with pain?

______________________________ **2 ■ 0**

16. Why doesn't the bear simply let the pot fall off its head?

______________________________ **2 ■ 0**

Look at Paragraphs 11 to 14.

17. Which **three** words tell us the bear makes a great deal of noise because it cannot see properly? **2 1 0**

(i) ______________________________

(ii) ______________________________

(iii) ______________________________

18. Give **two** reasons for the children's laughter. **2 1 0**

(i) ______________________________

(ii) ______________________________

Marks

Think about the passage as a whole.

19. In Paragraph 1 we are told that the story took place in 1843.

Write down three other pieces of information which suggest that it happened a long time ago. 2 1 0

(i) ______________________________

(ii) ______________________________

(iii) ______________________________

20. Read the following statements and then tick (✓) to show whether each is **TRUE**, **FALSE** or **CANNOT TELL** from the passage.

	TRUE	FALSE	CANNOT TELL	Marks
When he stood up, the bear's nose almost touched the loft.				2 ■ 0
The father of the family had gone hunting.				2 ■ 0
Agnes had dark hair with curls.				2 ■ 0
Afterwards, everyone laughed except the mother.				2 ■ 0

21. Apart from giving instructions to the family, what else shows that Lyddie is a responsible and capable girl? Give **two** examples. 2 1 0

(i) ______________________________

(ii) ______________________________

[*END OF QUESTION PAPER*]

1997
WEDNESDAY, 7 MAY
10.50 AM – 11.40 AM

ENGLISH
STANDARD GRADE
Foundation Level
Reading
Text

Read carefully the passage. It will help if you read it twice. When you have done so, answer the questions. Use the spaces provided in the Question/Answer booklet.

The following article has been adapted from "The Scotsman".

Close encounter of the Mir kind

CHRIS ROGERS of *Newsround* joins in a thrilling link-up with a space station.

1 SCHOOLCHILDREN from all over Europe have taken part in an exciting three days of learning all about space travel — and their teachers were real astronauts, speaking to them from space!

2 The children were chosen from the 14 member countries of the European Space Agency, which was set up in 1980 to put European missions into space. Representing Britain were pupils from Blue Coat School, Coventry, and Kemnal Technology College, Kent. A live link-up with Russia's Mir space station was established at Disneyland, Paris. I was there too, to join the 600 children who touched down at Paris for the weekend of space events

3 One pupil per country was chosen to question the astronauts on the Mir space station, which is orbiting nearly 200 miles above the Earth. The station was launched to enable long-term experiments to be carried out. Two Russian astronauts on board have been joined by a German.

4 Peter Worden from Kemnal College put the question for Britain. He asked about the worst aspects of space travel . . . "because everything everyone says about space seems to be good", he told me later. "There must be bad things and I want to know them."

5 Every pupil from the chosen schools had to choose a question they wanted to ask the astronauts and then submit it to the organisers at Disneyland. Peter's question was picked, so how did he feel? "Nervous, but I'm more nervous about being live on French television and fluffing my question up," he replied.

6 Throughout the morning, children spoke to other astronauts on the ground and took part in various activities which taught them about the space missions so far. But at midday came the moment everyone had been waiting for and the image of the three Mir astronauts appeared on huge screens.

7 There were claps and cheering as it became clear we had connected with the space station, but there was silence from the screens. "Hello, Mir, can you hear us? It's Paris here," the French presenter shouted — still there was silence.

The Mir space station, orbiting nearly 200 miles above the Earth.

8 Then, a faint voice could be heard from the speakers and there were more cheers. "Yes, hello Paris, we can hear you now." The looks on the children's faces said it all. We had indeed made contact with three brave men, alone in space.

9 The presenter invited the various children to ask their questions. One from Norway asked what they could see in space now. The astronaut replied, "Well, I'll point the camera out of the window so you can see." After a while it became clear that we were looking at planet Earth, with the sun just a momentary glimmer of orange light at the edge of our small planet, followed by total darkness.

10 Then it was Peter's turn. "What's the worst aspect of being in space?"

11 "The feeling of weightlessness is just smashing, fantastic, but it causes many problems," the astronaut replied. "There are some difficulties and life is not easy in space."

12 After the link-up, a spectacular space show rounded off the weekend's activities. Everyone who took part in the weekend seemed to have a special experience to take home with them. One Irish boy told me, "It was great to talk to astronauts in space, something I've always wanted to do."

13 Stephanie from France had a more serious memory of the event. "Being able to talk to people in space is very important for us. We are interested in science and our century is the century of science."

14 As we left the park to go back to the comforts of home we couldn't help but spare a thought for those astronauts. Life in space seemed tough — you even have to go to the toilet upside down!

[*END OF PASSAGE*]

Marks

QUESTIONS

Write your answers in the spaces provided.

Look at Paragraphs 1 and 2.

1. Where did the children who took part in the weekend of events come from?

______________________________ 2 ■ 0

2. What did they learn about?

______________________________ 2 1 0

3. (*a*) What **two** things were unusual about their teachers? 2 1 0

(i) ______________________________

(ii) ______________________________

(*b*) How does the writer's punctuation in Paragraph 1 help to show that the teachers were unusual?

______________________________ 2 ■ 0

4. Complete the following sentences about the events.

(*a*) The pupils representing Britain came from

____

and ______________________________ 2 1 0

(*b*) The live link-up connected

____

with ______________________________ 2 1 0

Marks

5. (*a*) **Write down** the expression which the writer uses to describe the children's arrival in Paris.

______________________________ 2 ■ 0

(*b*) Why is this a particularly suitable expression to use here?

____

______________________________ 2 1 0

Look at Paragraphs 3 to 5.

6. What is the purpose of the Mir space station?

____

______________________________ 2 1 0

7. Why did Peter Worden want to know about the "worst aspects of space travel" (Paragraph 4)?

____

______________________________ 2 1 0

8. Who chose the final questions?

______________________________ 2 ■ 0

9. Give **two** reasons why Peter was nervous. 2 1 0

(i) ______________________________

(ii) ______________________________

Marks

Look at Paragraphs 6 and 7.

10. What **two** things did the children do in the morning?

(i) ______________________________ 2 1 0

(ii) ______________________________ 2 1 0

11. (*a*) What was the **first** sign that the link-up had been made?

____

______________________________ 2 1 0

(*b*) How did the crowd react?

______________________________ 2 1 0

(*c*) What made the situation more tense?

______________________________ 2 ■ 0

Look at Paragraphs 8 and 9.

12. "The looks on the children's faces said it all." (Paragraph 8)

What sort of looks do you think were on their faces?

______________________________ 2 ■ 0

13. How did the astronaut answer the question from Norway?

____

______________________________ 2 1 0

Look at Paragraphs 12 and 13.

14. **Write down one** word which the writer uses to show that the **final event** of the weekend was impressive.

2 ■ 0

Marks

15. The weekend was a "special experience" for those who took part. (Paragraph 12)

Why was talking to the astronauts special for: **2 1 0**

(i) the Irish boy? ______________________________

____

(ii) the French girl? ______________________________

____

Think about the passage as a whole.

16. At times, the writer makes us feel sorry for the astronauts in space.

Write down two examples of this. **2 1 0**

(i) ______________________________

(ii) ______________________________

17. Read the following statements and then tick (✓) to show whether each is **TRUE**, **FALSE** or **CANNOT TELL** from the passage.

	TRUE	FALSE	CANNOT TELL	Marks
The Mir space station has been in orbit since 1980.				2 ■ 0
Two of the astronauts were German and one was Russian.				2 ■ 0
Fourteen pupils were chosen to ask the astronauts questions.				2 ■ 0
The link-up with the astronauts took place at night.				2 ■ 0
The astronauts enjoyed the feeling of weightlessness.				2 ■ 0

Marks

18. This article was taken from a newspaper.

(*a*) **Write down three** features of it which are typical of a newspaper article. **2 1 0**

(i) ______________________________

(ii) ______________________________

(iii) ______________________________

(*b*) Explain how any **one** of these features helped you to enjoy the article.

____

____

______________________________ **2 [redacted] 0**

19. Imagine you had been at the "weekend of space events". (Paragraph 2)

Which event or activity mentioned in the article do you think you would remember best?

Give a reason for your choice.

____

____

____

______________________________ **2 1 0**

[*END OF QUESTION PAPER*]

1998
WEDNESDAY, 6 MAY
10.50 AM – 11.40 AM

ENGLISH
STANDARD GRADE
Foundation Level
Reading
Text

Read carefully the passage overleaf. It will help if you read it twice. When you have done so, answer the questions. Use the spaces provided in the Question/Answer booklet.

First Jump

1 After breakfast on a bright, sunny morning, they paraded on the square, each group under its sergeant. Herded aboard trucks, the whole company was transported to Baldoon Aerodrome, where the men were to do their jumps. No one spoke much as they turned from the road and passed a sentry at the gate. Even the high-spirited Tam Devlin crouched down in a corner, with nothing to say for himself.

2 "We're first to jump," Sergeant Bolton informed his group. "Five men will go up with me in ten minutes' time. Hold yourself in readiness."

3 Alex could not still the tremor in his legs as he sat on the grass, waiting until the sergeant returned. His mouth felt like an oven that had long since overheated. Time and again, he looked up into the sky and asked himself why he had volunteered for the paratroops.

4 "Kennedy, Rae, Devlin, Anderson and Myles, follow me!" Sergeant Bolton beckoned to the men in question.

5 Forcing himself to walk steadily, Alex followed the sergeant's lean form to where an enormous balloon hung anchored to the ground. An officer and a corporal handed out parachutes, then ushered the six men into an open cage which was suspended below the balloon.

6 "Five hundred feet, Sergeant!" The officer slammed an iron gate. "I'll fire a Very light when everything's ready down here."

7 "There's nothing to it, lads." Bolton tried to put them at ease. "Dropping drill first though. You will jump one after the other from fixed lines. Each man will make sure that the man in front of him has fastened his line properly. Normally, a man will make certain himself—when his life depends upon it. But we rigidly adhere to the rule that each man will check the man in front."

8 "What about the last man, Sergeant?" Pate Rae's voice betrayed the tension within him.

9 "I'll be here to see to the last man." Bolton spoke easily. "No matter where, or when, you jump, there will always be a dispatcher, who will see to the last man."

10 "We're going up!" Snack Kennedy shouted in alarm. "The balloon's going up!"

11 Under the control of a winch, the balloon ascended into the heavens, carrying its cargo of nervous men. Alex watched the ground fall away from beneath them. White-faced and with his hands gripped tightly around an iron support, he closed his eyes and prayed for the courage to jump when the time came.

12 "Fasten lines!" Bolton's command seemed to come from a very long distance. "Myles! You will go first."

13 Fumbling and shaking, they fastened the safety-clips to a rail above their heads. Its brightness dimmed by the sun, a Very light sizzled into the sky.

14 "Ready!" Bolton smiled. "Take it easy, Myles. I've seen a thousand drop from this balloon and never an accident yet. When you do jump, don't look down—keep your eyes fixed on the sky: it's better that way. Get set!" The sergeant lifted an iron guard rail. "When I say go—jump!"

15 It took a tremendous effort on Alex's part not to turn his eyes downwards as he stood teetering on the edge of the five-hundred foot drop. Fixing his gaze on a woolly cloud high above him, he waited for the order that would launch him into space.

16 "Go!" The command thundered through his whole being.

17 A violent slap on the back and he was falling downwards at a terrific speed. Something between a sob and a scream issued from his throat as he caught a fleeting impression of the earth spinning beneath him. There came a tremendous jerk around his middle and he was floating gently in mid-air, shroud lines taut over his head. A sensation of complete satisfaction almost overwhelmed him.

18 "It's easy!" Tears of relief flowed down his cheeks.

19 Alex would have willingly stayed in the pleasant position of floating between Heaven and Earth, but, all too soon, the green grass rushed up towards him at a tremendous speed. Remembering all he had been taught about how to fall, he relaxed every muscle in his body and prepared to make contact with the earth. He did not make a "banana"—as a bad landing was termed by the older hands who wore the red beret. Immediately his boots touched the grass, Alex rolled to one side, allowed the billowing silk canopy to settle down, then hurriedly gathered it in before a gust of wind could drag him across the aerodrome. He stood for a minute with all the emotion drained from his body. His first jump was over and it wasn't so bad, other than that brief second before the parachute opened. Folding the silk as well as he could, Alex watched his companions make their jumps. Everyone landed easily and seemed to be quite happy that, at last, they were past the stumbling-block of their first jump.

Adapted from *Dropping Zone* by P. Baillie

[*END OF PASSAGE*]

Marks

QUESTIONS

Write your answers in the spaces provided.

Look at Paragraphs 1 and 2.

1. **Write down two** words from the first paragraph that tell you this passage is about soldiers.

   2 1 0

2. Where were the soldiers going and what **exactly** were they going to do there?

   2 1 0

3. The soldiers were "Herded aboard trucks". What **two** things are suggested by the word "Herded"?

   2 1 0

   (i)

   (ii)

4. (*a*) **Write down** an expression from **Paragraph 1** that tells you the soldiers were worried.

   2 [redacted] 0

   (*b*) Explain fully what Tam Devlin was like **normally**.

   2 1 0

Marks

Look at Paragraphs 3 to 6.

5. Explain fully how you can tell that Alex was as nervous as the other men.

____

____ 2 1 0

6. From the information given in **Paragraphs 4 and 5**, which **one** of these statements is **true**?

A Alex was the second in command of the group.

B Alex helped to give out the parachutes.

C Alex's second name was Kennedy, Rae, Devlin, Anderson or Myles.

D Alex was the first man aboard the balloon.

Write down the correct letter in the box below.

☐

2 ■ 0

7. **Write down three** things that Alex noticed about the balloon. 2 1 0

(i) ____

(ii) ____

(iii) ____

8. (*a*) In **Paragraph 6**, why has the writer placed an exclamation mark at the end of the officer's statement, "Five hundred feet, Sergeant!"?

____

____ 2 ■ 0

(*b*) Why has he put a capital letter at the beginning of the word "Very"?

____

____ 2 ■ 0

Marks

Look at Paragraphs 7 to 10.

9. (*a*) What **two** things tell you that Sergeant Bolton **knew** his men were worried about the jump? 2 1 0

(i) ______

______

(ii) ______

______

(*b*) **Write down** the expression that tells you that Sergeant Bolton's efforts to make the men relax were **not** working with Rae.

______ 2 ■ 0

10. What **exactly** was the job of "a dispatcher"?

______

______

______ 2 1 0

Look at Paragraphs 11 to 14.

11. **Write down** an expression from **Paragraph 11** that suggests the balloon went very high into the air.

______ 2 ■ 0

12. **Write down** any **two** things Alex did which showed that he was afraid **as the balloon went up**. 2 1 0

(i) ______

(ii) ______

Marks

13. How did Sergeant Bolton know that the balloon had reached 500 feet?

____

____ **2 ■ 0**

14. Sergeant Bolton tried several ways to put Myles at his ease.
Write down two of them. **2 1 0**

(i) ____________________________________

(ii) ____________________________________

Look at Paragraphs 15 to 18.

15. (*a*) **Write down** an expression from **Paragraph 15** that emphasises the dangerous position Alex was in.

____ **2 ■ 0**

(*b*) Explain fully how we know that, in spite of the danger, Alex remembered the Sergeant's advice.

____

____ **2 1 0**

16. **Write down** an expression that suggests Alex may have needed help to jump.

____ **2 ■ 0**

17. What caused the "tremendous jerk"?

____ **2 1 0**

Marks

18. The following words describe feelings:

terror   relief   fear

Using each word only once, complete the following sentences.

(i) In **Paragraph 15**, Alex's main feeling was ______________________. 2 ■ 0

(ii) At the **beginning of Paragraph 17**, Alex's main feeling was __________. 2 ■ 0

(iii) At the **end of Paragraph 17**, Alex's main feeling was ______________. 2 ■ 0

Look at Paragraph 19.

19. **Write down two** expressions which suggest that Alex would have liked the trip to the ground to last longer. 2 1 0

(i) ____

(ii) ____

20. What are the **two** most important things a paratrooper must do in order to fall properly? 2 1 0

(i) ____

____

(ii) ____

____

21. Why did Alex have to gather in his parachute quickly?

____

____

____ 2 1 0

Marks

Think about the passage as a whole.

22. Why is the first jump described as a "stumbling-block" (Paragraph 19)?

2 1 0

23. Using evidence from the passage, explain how **you** would have felt in Alex's position.

2 1 0

[*END OF QUESTION PAPER*]

SCOTTISH CERTIFICATE OF EDUCATION 1999

FRIDAY, 30 APRIL
10.30 AM – 11.40 AM

ENGLISH
STANDARD GRADE
Foundation Level
Reading
Text

Read carefully the passage overleaf. It will help if you read it twice. When you have done so, answer the questions. Use the spaces provided in the Question/Answer booklet.

The following passage has been adapted from "The Independent".

"Thank God . . . it's a miracle"

Shipwrecked Briton was losing hope of rescue

1 It was the thud of an Australian fist on the carbon hull of Tony Bullimore's overturned yacht that told him he was not going to die.

2 The British yachtsman had spent four days and four nights in an air-pocket inside his capsized yacht, praying that he would be saved. "I started shouting, 'I'm coming, I'm coming,'" he said. "It took a few seconds to get from one end of the boat to the other. Then I took a few deep breaths and I dived out of the boat."

3 It was the climax of one of the most dramatic sea rescues of all time—and a heroic survival in a cabin perched on boxes with "a little chocolate and a little water" and three feet of seawater lapping around him.

4 The Briton had been stranded in one of the most treacherous parts of the world, more than 1,500 miles from the Australian coast and 900 miles from Antarctica.

The conditions in which he had existed were the stuff of nightmares—solitude, pitch darkness, and absolute silence save for the sound of icy waters sloshing round his feet. 5

"It was heaven . . . I really never thought I would reach that far."

Tossed around by giant waves, he nibbled pieces of chocolate and took breaths from a diminishing air supply. 6

When Bullimore emerged into daylight early yesterday morning, the moment was almost spiritual. "It was heaven, absolute heaven," he said. "I really never thought I would reach that far. I was starting to look back over my life and was thinking, 'Well, 7

I've had a good life, I've done most of the things I had wanted to.' If I was picking words to describe it, it would be a miracle, an absolute miracle."

8 Bullimore said he felt he had been "born all over again" and as he began his new life yesterday, heading back to land on board the Australian frigate, HMAS *Adelaide*, he had plenty of opportunity to thank those who had saved him. *Adelaide's* skipper, Captain Raydon Gates, said the rescued sailor's first words had been "Thank God" and "It's a miracle."

9 The Australian rescue team was first alerted to the Briton's plight on Sunday, when a satellite distress signal was picked up from his yacht, *Exide Challenger*. Winds of up to 55 knots had snapped the boat's keel and capsized it. To the very last, the rescuers were not sure whether Bullimore was still on board, or floating on a life-raft, or lost for ever.

10 Thierry Dubois, a French yachtsman who like Bullimore was a competitor in the Vendee Globe round-the-world race, had also sent a distress signal from the same area.

11 In extreme weather conditions, an Australian Orion spotter plane scoured the icy expanse of the Southern Ocean for the two men and the HMAS *Adelaide* began its long rescue voyage from Perth, eventually picking up Dubois from a life-raft on Wednesday evening.

12 Inside *Exide Challenger*, Bullimore was doing his best to help the rescue. From his perch in an air-pocket at the top of the boat's upturned hull, he repeatedly dived into the icy waters to harness his life-raft so that it would not drift away and deceive the rescuers.

13 On Tuesday, however, the rescue operation was distracted when one of Bullimore's emergency beacons was detected some distance from the yacht. But the rescuers continued to hope that the yachtsman had remained with his craft.

14 At 1 am GMT yesterday, shortly after daybreak in the Southern Ocean, *Adelaide* reached the stricken yacht which had been sighted on Tuesday by the spotter plane but with no sign of life.

Some of the crew were dispatched in a 15
dinghy and Bullimore heard first the knocking on the hull and then the sound of voices. Plunging once again into the freezing waters, he swam for 15 seconds through the darkness before emerging from beneath the yacht. Captain Gates said, "When he bobbed up alongside the yacht, it was a tremendously exciting feeling throughout the ship."

At Bullimore's home in Bristol, news of the 16
rescue was greeted with the popping of champagne corks and tears of joy. "The old dog is alive. He's bloomin' alive," said his wife, Lalel. She said that, despite the terrible anxiety of the past few days, she knew she could not stop her "stubborn" husband going to sea again. "He's his own man. He will do what he wants to do. If he thinks he's got to go on, then he goes on," she said.

Although rescue co-ordinators in Australia 17
said yesterday that they were not counting the cost of the operation, it is likely to be in the region of £1m. *Exide Challenger*, valued at £500,000, has been abandoned to a watery grave.

Ian Burrell

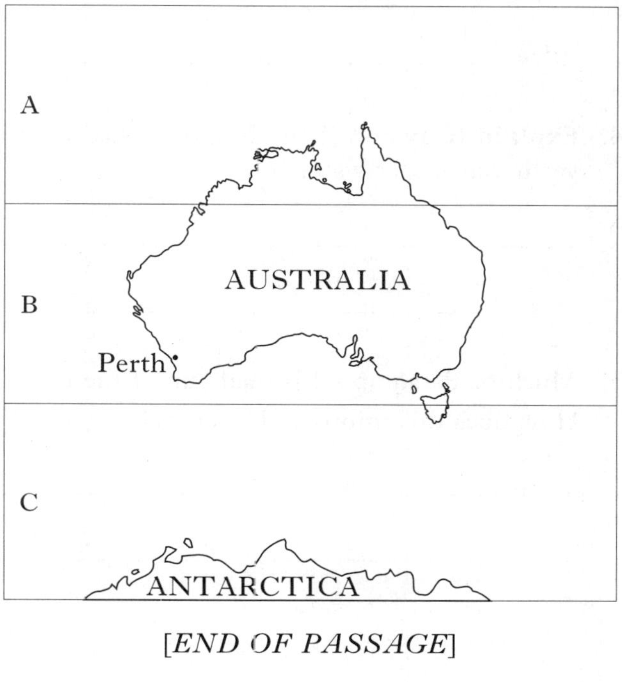

[*END OF PASSAGE*]

Marks

QUESTIONS

Write your answers in the spaces provided.

Look at the general layout of this passage.

1. What **features of the layout** make it obvious that it comes from a newspaper?

____

____ 2 1 0

2. **Look at the headline.**

   (*a*) In what **two** ways is it typical of newspaper headlines? 2 1 0

   (i) ____

   (ii) ____

   (*b*) Why are there inverted commas around the words **"Thank God . . . it's a miracle"**?

   ____ 2 ■ 0

Look at Paragraphs 1 and 2.

3. Write down **two** separate expressions that suggest Tony Bullimore was in trouble. 2 1 0

   (i) ____

   (ii) ____

4. **Explain fully** how Tony Bullimore had been able to breathe even though most of his yacht was under water.

____

____ 2 1 0

5. Much of Paragraph 2 is made up of the actual words spoken by Tony Bullimore. How does this improve the report?

____

____ 2 ■ 0

Marks

Look at Paragraphs 3, 4 and 5.

6. ". . . one of the most dramatic sea rescues of all time . . ." (Paragraph 3)

(*a*) Reporters often use sensational, exaggerated language like this.
Write down two other examples from paragraphs 3–5. **2 1 0**

(i) ______________________________

(ii) ______________________________

(*b*) **Write down two facts** given in **Paragraph 4** that suggest this rescue might well have been ". . . one of the most dramatic . . ." ever. **2 1 0**

(i) ______________________________

(ii) ______________________________

7. What were the frightening conditions in which Bullimore existed after the yacht overturned?

____

____

______________________________ **2 1 0**

Look at Paragraphs 6 and 7.

8. ". . . he nibbled pieces of chocolate . . ."
Why does the writer use the word "nibbled" here?
Give **two** reasons. **2 1 0**

(i) ______________________________

(ii) ______________________________

Marks

9. (*a*) Which **one** of the following words best describes Bullimore's **attitude** when he thought he was **not** going to survive? Tick (✓) the box.

ACCEPTANCE	
REGRET	
RESENTMENT	
PANIC	

(*b*) Give a reason for your answer.

____

____ **2 1 0**

Look at Paragraphs 8, 9 and 10.

10. ". . . on board the Australian frigate, HMAS *Adelaide* . . ." (Paragraph 8)
Why is the word "*Adelaide*" written in italics?

____ **2 ■ 0**

11. (*a*) How did the Australian rescue team first realise Bullimore was in trouble?

____

____ **2 ■ 0**

(*b*) What **three** possibilities did the rescuers then have to consider? **2 1 0**

(i) ____________________________________

(ii) ____________________________________

(iii) ____________________________________

Marks

12. Why was Bullimore in that area in the first place?

____

____ **2 ■ 0**

Look at Paragraphs 11, 12 and 13.

13. From these paragraphs write down: **2 1 0**

(i) the **one** word that suggests the thoroughness of the search;

(ii) the **one** word that suggests the size of the area to be searched.

14. Why was Bullimore so anxious to keep the life-raft tied to his boat?
Give **two** reasons. **2 1 0**

(i) ____

(ii) ____

15. Why, despite Bullimore's efforts, was the rescue party almost fooled?
Give **two** reasons. **2 1 0**

(i) ____

(ii) ____

Marks

Look at Paragraphs 14 to 17.

16. How did the rescuers get close to Bullimore's yacht?

2 ■ 0

17. What were the reactions of Bullimore's family to the news of his rescue?

2 1 0

18. Why does Mrs Bullimore describe her husband as "stubborn"?

2 ■ 0

Think about the passage as a whole.

19. Look at the illustration.

Why has a drawing been used rather than a photograph?

2 1 0

20. Look at the map.

It has been divided into three sections: A, B and C.

In the box provided, **indicate the section** in which you think the rescue took place and then, in the space below the box, **explain fully** why you think so.

2 1 0

[*END OF QUESTION PAPER*]

NATIONAL QUALIFICATIONS 2000

TUESDAY, 16 MAY
10.35 AM – 11.25 AM

ENGLISH
STANDARD GRADE
Foundation Level
Reading
Text

Read carefully the passage. It will help if you read it twice. When you have done so, answer the questions. Use the spaces provided in the Question/Answer booklet.

Adapted from an article by Audrey Ronning Topping.

Charlie, Our Mad, Bad Cockatoo

With a gleam in his eye and mischief in mind, he had us all under his spell.

1 I first met Charlie on Cat Street in Hong Kong. I was browsing for antiques when I heard a terrible screech and turned to see a beggar squatting on the kerb beside a balding, scruffy, white cockatoo.

2 Chained to a wooden perch, the bird was surrounded by children who were teasing him with sticks. The children laughed when the half-crazed creature snapped back at them with his hooked beak, flared his yellow crest and shrieked in Chinese. I was overcome with admiration. This little creature was a fighter.

3 I wanted to rescue him but could not bear the thought of keeping a bird in a cage. As I started to walk away, the cockatoo looked at me imploringly and said, "OK, OK, OK."

4 I was hooked. How did he know I spoke English? After some haggling, I bought him.

5 At home, I removed his shackle. He was grateful and, dog-like, began following me round the flat. He couldn't fly because the beggar had cut his flight feathers, so he waddled like a duck and used his beak and claws to hoist himself up our potted trees.

6 In the wild, baby cockatoos learn survival from their parents and other members of the flock. Now, in captivity, Charlie began imitating the only flock he knew, my family.

7 Charlie had a remarkably quick mind and good memory and was soon calling us by name.

8 Every day he picked up new words. His first phrase was "Hello Charlie" and then "Hello" to anyone within range, then "Shut the door!" which soon became "Robin, go back and shut the door."

9 His most frequent word was "Why?" Often when I spoke to the children, Charlie would ask "Why?" just as they did. It drove me crazy. I finally shouted back, "Because I'm your mother!" That became his next phrase.

10 Before long we could see the results of our love and care. Charlie's feathers grew thick and glossy. He developed a confident glint in his eye and established himself as top of the pecking order with our four cats who, to my amazement, restrained their killer instincts even when Charlie stole their food.

11 We were convinced he would never fly again. But one day, after months of watching the children play in the courtyard below the flat, he suddenly dived off the balcony, glided eight storeys down on his crippled wings and made a three-point landing—claws and beak—on the shoulder of Susan.

12 The surprised children shouted, "Super Charlie!" and swung him round in circles on the end of a long stick. He loved it. Soon he called out "Super Charlie" each time he landed in the courtyard.

13 When we moved to Scarsdale, New York State, Charlie became an instant celebrity, greeting everyone with "Hello there! How ya doing?"

14 He slept in the kitchen, where he acted as watchbird, but spent most of his time in an old apple tree in the garden. There he hacked out a large apartment for himself with two entrances and several peepholes. Charlie could not fly up or take off without help, but in the mornings he would hoist himself up with his beak and claws, and glide from tree to tree. In the evening he would call "Audrey!" or "Robin!" until one of us came to bring him inside.

15 Charlie spoke English to us and Spanish to our housekeeper. He meowed to the cats and barked and whistled to our three dogs. They came obediently when he called, and guarded him from stray animals in the garden.

16 Unlike the other members of our family, he was a good listener. We were convinced he could understand everything we said. He could keep a secret, too, so we spilled out all our problems to him. I encouraged this because he was cheaper than a psychiatrist. Eventually we began to think of Charlie as a person of importance.

17 Before I knew it, 25 years had passed.

18 One clear blue Sunday afternoon we prepared a barbecue in the garden for Joanna's birthday. Charlie was perched on the top branch of a tall tree, with about 20 fat crows he hung out with. They had become friends over the years—Charlie spoke fluent crow and allowed them to share his apples.

19 Surrounded by his crows, Charlie was in his element. Every few minutes he would hang upside down by one leg, flap his wings and shout, "Super Charlie!"

20 Suddenly the calm was shattered by his screams. We looked up to see two large hawks diving out of the sky, straight for Charlie. One hawk grabbed him in its talons and began to fly away.

21 The crows took off after the invading hawks like fighter planes attacking a bomber, cawing to signal other crows to join them. They soon formed a thick black cloud above the hawks and prevented them from gaining height.

22 The evil birdnappers flew out of the garden and headed across a busy street. Joanna and I ran below, shouting and flailing with sticks while the crows flew above, circling and dive-bombing. Motorists screeched to a halt.

23 Finally the crows forced the hawk into a tree. We watched in astonishment as Charlie escaped while his winged allies held the enemy at bay.

24 For one glorious minute, he really was Super Charlie. In his heroic battle, he at last flew high—like the free spirit he was meant to be.

25 Then the second hawk rocketed down, snatching him from above. We heard one last scream. Dear Charlie. He died a champion.

26 That evening, the birthday celebration became a funeral as the whole family gathered to pay respects to one of our own. We saved a few yellow crest feathers and buried him in the garden.

27 Charlie was composed of the stuff that legends are made of, and in our family he has become just that. None of us will ever forget the adventures we shared for 25 years with Charlie Cockatoo.

[*END OF PASSAGE*]

QUESTIONS

Write your answers in the spaces provided.

Look at Paragraphs 1 and 2.

1. What first drew the writer's attention to Charlie?

____ 2 0

2. **Write down two** things which show that Charlie was not well looked after by the beggar.

(i) ____ 2 1

(ii) ____ 0

3. "This little creature was a fighter." (Paragraph 2)

(*a*) **Write down three separate words** the writer uses to describe how Charlie reacted when the children teased him.

2 1 0

(*b*) How did this behaviour make the writer feel about Charlie? 2 1

____ 0

Look at Paragraphs 3 and 4.

4. (*a*) Why did the writer not rescue Charlie immediately?

____

____ 2 0

(*b*) What **two** things persuaded her to rescue him?

(i) ____ 2 1

(ii) ____ 0

5. **Write down** the expression which tells us that the writer did not pay as much as the beggar asked for Charlie.

____ 2 0

Look at Paragraph 5.

6. Explain fully why Charlie began following the writer "doglike" round the flat.

____ 2 1 0

____

7. Explain fully why Charlie had to use his beak and claws to "hoist himself up our potted trees".

____ 2 1 0

____

Look at Paragraphs 6 to 9.

8. **Write down** the word which the writer uses to compare her family to Charlie's family in the wild.

[ ] 2 0

9. What did Charlie do which showed he had "a remarkably quick mind and good memory"? (Paragraph 7)

____ 2 1 0

____

Look at Paragraphs 10 to 12.

10. How did Charlie's **appearance** and **behaviour** change as a result of the family's love and care?

____

____ **2**

1

____ **0**

11. Explain clearly what was amazing about the cats' attitude to Charlie.

____ **2**

1

____ **0**

12. Explain fully why the children were "surprised". (Paragraph 12)

____ **2**

1

____ **0**

Look at Paragraphs 13 and 14.

13. Despite becoming an "instant celebrity" (Paragraph 13), what things does Charlie do which remind us he is a bird?

____ **2**

1

____ **0**

Look at Paragraphs 15 and 16.

14. Explain why the family "began to think of Charlie as a person of importance".

____ **2**

1

____ **0**

Look at Paragraph 17.

15. Why do you think the writer has made this sentence a short paragraph on its own?

____ 2 0

Look at Paragraphs 18 and 19.

16. Explain fully how Charlie and the crows had become friends.

____ 2

____ 1 0

17. " . . . Charlie was in his element."

Explain how the rest of Paragraph 19 helps you to understand the meaning of this expression

____ 2 1

____ 0

Look at Paragraphs 20 to 23.

18. (*a*) **Write down three** expressions the writer uses to make the attack seem warlike.

(i) ____

(ii) ____ 2 1

(iii) ____ 0

(*b*) Choose any **one** of these expressions and **explain how well** you think it helps to describe what happened.

____ 2

____ 0

19. "Motorists screeched to a halt." (Paragraph 22)
What **two** things caused this?

(i) ______________________________ 2 1 0

(ii) ______________________________

Look at Paragraphs 24 to 27.

20. **Write down** the word which shows how fast the second hawk moved.

[ ] 2 0

21. "For one glorious minute, he really was Super Charlie." (Paragraph 24)
Which expression in this paragraph explains why the writer thought this?

______________________________ 2 0

Think about the passage as a whole.

22. Read the following statements and then tick (✓) to show whether each is TRUE, FALSE or CANNOT TELL from the passage.

	TRUE	FALSE	CANNOT TELL	
The Toppings lived in Hong Kong for 25 years.				2 0
The Topping family had three dogs and four cats.				2 0
Charlie died on a Saturday afternoon.				2 0

23. "None of us will ever forget the adventures we shared for 25 years with Charlie Cockatoo." (Paragraph 27)
Which adventure do you think is most memorable and why?

____

______________________________ 2 1 0

____

[*END OF QUESTION PAPER*]

1994
MONDAY 9 MAY
1.00 PM – 1.50 PM

ENGLISH
STANDARD GRADE
General Level
Reading
Text

Read carefully the passage. It will help if you read it twice. When you have done so, answer the questions. Use the spaces provided in the Question/Answer booklet.

1994

In this extract, the writer describes his return to Spain during the Spanish Civil War, the welcome he receives there and the surprising outcome.

1 In December 1937 I crossed the Pyrenees from France—two days on foot through the snow. I don't know why I chose December; it was just one of a number of idiocies I committed at the time. But on the second night, near the frontier, I was guided over the last peak by a shepherd and directed down a path to a small mountain farmhouse.

2 It was dark when I reached it—a boulder among boulders—and I knocked on the door, which was presently opened by a young man with a rifle. He held up a lantern to my face and studied me closely, and I saw that he was wearing the armband of the Republican side.

3 "I've come to join you," I said.

4 The young man slung his rifle over his shoulder and motioned me to enter the hut. A dark passage led to a smoky room. Inside, in a group, stood an old man and woman, another youth with a gun, and a gaunt little girl about eleven years old. They were huddled together like a family photograph fixing me with glassy teeth-set smiles.

5 There was a motionless silence while they took me in—seeing a young tattered stranger, coatless, soaked to the knees and carrying a kit-bag from which a violin bow protruded. Suddenly the old woman said "Ay!" and beckoned me to the fire, which was piled high with glowing pine cones. I crouched, thawing out by the choking fumes, sensing deeply this moment of arrival.

6 "Will you eat?" asked the woman.

7 "Don't be mad," said her husband.

8 He cleared part of the table, and the old woman gave me a spoon and a plate. At the other end the little girl was cleaning a gun, frowning, tongue out, as though doing her homework. An old black cooking-pot hung over the smouldering pine cones, from which the woman ladled me out some soup. It was hot, though thin, a watery mystery that might have been the tenth boiling of the bones of a hare. As I ate, my clothes steaming, shivering and warming up, the boys knelt by the doorway, hugging their rifles and watching me. Everybody watched me except for the gun-cleaning girl who was intent on more urgent matters. But I could not, from my appearance, offer much of a threat.

9 Gradually, a light joky whispering seemed to fill the room. "What are you?"

10 "I'm English."

11 "Ah, yes—he's English."

12 They nodded to each other with grave politeness.

13 "And how did you come here?"

14 "I came over the mountain."

15 "Yes, he walked over the mountain ... on foot."

16 They were all round me at the table now as I ate my soup, all pulling at their eyes and winking, nodding delightedly and repeating everything I said, as though humouring a child just learning to speak.

17 "He's come to join us," said one of the youths; and that set them off again, and even the girl lifted her gaunt head and simpered. But I was pleased too, pleased that I managed to get here so easily after two days' wandering among peaks and blizzards. I was here now with friends.

18 The people in the kitchen were a people stripped for war—the men smoking beech leaves, the soup reduced to near water; around us hand-grenades hanging on the walls like strings of onions, muskets and cartridge-belts piled in the corner, and open orange-boxes packed with silver bullets like fish. War was still so local then, it was like stepping into another room. And this was what I had come to re-visit. But I was now awash with sleep, hearing the blurred murmuring of voices and feeling the rocks of Spain under my feet. The men's eyes grew narrower, watching the unexpected stranger, and his lumpy belongings drying by the fire.

19 Then the old woman came and took me by the elbow and led me upstairs and one of the boys followed close behind. I was shown into a small windowless room of bare whitewashed stone containing a large iron bed smothered with goatskins. I lay down exhausted, and the old woman put an oil lamp on the floor, placed a cold hand on my brow, and left me with a gruff good-night. The room had no door, just an opening in the wall, and the boy stretched himself languidly across the threshold. He lay on his side, his chin resting on the stock of his gun, watching me with large black unblinking eyes. As I slipped into sleep I remembered I had left all my baggage downstairs; but it didn't seem to matter now.

20 I was awoken early next morning by the two armed brothers who were dressed for outdoors in ponchos of rabbit skin. They gave me a bucket of snow to wash in, then led me gingerly downstairs and sat me on a stool where the old lady poured me some coffee. The little girl, her hair brushed and shining already, was fitting ammunition into cartridge-belts. As I drank my coffee—which tasted of rusty buttons—she looked at me with radiant slyness.

21 "He came over the mountains," she said perkily, nodding to herself. The boys giggled, and the old man coughed. They brought me my baggage and helped me sling it over my shoulders, and told me that a horse and cart were waiting for me outside.

22 Then the boys half-marched me into the lane and the rest of the family followed and stood watching, blowing on their purple fingers. The old woman and child had bright shawls on their heads, while, for some reason, the old man wore a tall top hat. The boys helped me into the back of the cart and climbed up after me. The driver sniffed, and uncoiled his whip.

23 "Horse and cart," said one of the brothers, nudging me smartly. "We've got to save your legs. They must be half destroyed with all this walking over mountains. And what have we got if we haven't got your legs? You wouldn't be much use to us, would you?"

24 I was beginning to get a bit bored with all this levity, and sat there silent and shivering. The boys perched close beside me, one on each side, holding their guns at the ready, like sentries. Every so often they pointed them at me and nodded brightly. They appeared to be in a state of nervous high spirits. "Vamanos!" snarled the driver, and shook up the reins crossly. The old man and his wife raised their hands solemnly and told me to go with God. The little girl threw a stone at the horse, or it may have been at me, but it hit the horse and caused it to start with a jerk. So we began to lumber and creak down the steep rocky lane, the brothers now holding me by either elbow. The Pyrenees stood high behind us, white and hard, their peaks colouring to the rising sun. The boys nodded towards them, grinning, nudging me sharply again, and baring their chestnut-tinted teeth.

25 Through the iced winter morning, slipping over glassy rocks, we made our stumbling way down the valley, passing snow-covered villages, empty and bare, from which all life and sound seemed withdrawn. This chilling silence was surely not one of nature, which could be broken by a goat-bell or the chirp of a bird. It was as if paralysing pestilence had visited the place, and I was to notice it on a number of occasions in the weeks to come. It was simply the stupefying numbness of war.

26 After an hour or so we came to a small hill town still shuttered by the shadow of rocks. A bent woman crept by, bearing a great load of firewood. A cat shot through a hole in a wall. I noticed that the brothers had suddenly grown tense and anxious, sitting straight as pillars, thin-lipped, beside me. Two militiamen, in khaki ponchos, came out of a doorway and marched ahead of us down the street. Even our driver perked up and began to look around him with what appeared to be an air of importance. The militiamen led us into the square, to the dilapidated Town Hall, from which the Republican flag was hanging. The brothers called out to a couple of sentries who were sitting on the steps, and one of them got up and went inside. Now for a proper welcome, I thought. I got down from the cart, and the brothers followed. Then four soldiers came out with fixed bayonets.

27 "We've brought you the spy," said the brothers, and pushed me forward. The soldiers closed round me and handcuffed my wrists.

Adapted from *A Moment of War* by Laurie Lee

[*END OF PASSAGE*]

Marks

QUESTIONS

Write your answers in the spaces provided.

Look at Paragraph 1.

1. What difficulties did the writer face on his journey into Spain? **2 1 0**

(i) ______

(ii) ______

Look at Paragraph 2.

2. **Write down two** pieces of information which suggest that there was a war on. **2 1 0**

(i) ______

(ii) ______

Look at Paragraph 4.

3. Explain, **in your own words**, **two** ways in which the people seemed as if they were arranged for a "family photograph". **2 1 0**

(i) ______

(ii) ______

Look at Paragraphs 5 to 8.

4. Explain, **in your own words**, the effect in Paragraph 5 of the writer's appearance and possessions on the family.

______

______

______ **2 1 0**

5. The gun-cleaning girl was "intent on more urgent matters" (Paragraph 8).
Write down two words or expressions which show how intent she was. **2 1 0**

(i) ______

(ii) ______

Marks

6. The writer felt that his appearance couldn't "offer much of a threat" (Paragraph 8). Give **two** reasons why he should feel this way. **2 1 0**

(i) ______________________________

(ii) ______________________________

Look at Paragraphs 9 to 16.

7. At first, the family **seemed** to treat the writer seriously. What evidence is there that they **did not really believe** what he said?
Give **three** examples. **2 1 0**

(i) ______________________________

(ii) ______________________________

(iii) ______________________________

Look at Paragraph 18.

8. The people were "stripped for war".
In your own words, give **two** pieces of information which support this statement. **2 1 0**

(i) ______________________________

(ii) ______________________________

9. (*a*) Why is the expression "silver bullets like fish" a particularly suitable one for the writer to use in this situation?

____

____

______________________________ **2 1 0**

(*b*) **Write down** another expression from the same paragraph which conveys a similar idea.

______________________________ **2 [redacted] 0**

Marks

Look at Paragraph 19.

10. Why do you think the writer felt "it didn't seem to matter now" that he had left his baggage downstairs?

____

____ **2 1 0**

Look at Paragraphs 20 and 21.

11. Explain as fully as you can how the little girl's attitude towards the writer had changed from the previous day.

____

____

____ **2 1 0**

Look at Paragraphs 22 to 24.

12. "I was beginning to get a bit bored with all this levity" (Paragraph 24).
Explain **in your own words** what the writer means by this.

____

____ **2 1 0**

13. The brothers and the old couple treated the writer in a different way. **Explain the difference** as fully as you can. (You should refer to speech and behaviour.)

(*a*) The brothers ____

____

____ **2 1 0**

(*b*) The old couple _______________________________________

____

____ **2 1 0**

Marks

14. "The boys perched close beside me" (Paragraph 24).
The writer might have used "sat" rather than "perched". Explain why "perched" is a better word here.

2 1 0

Look at Paragraph 25.

15. What were the **two** effects on the villages of the "stupefying numbness of war"? 2 1 0

(i)

(ii)

Look at Paragraph 26.

16. **In your own words**, suggest one reason why the brothers had now grown "tense and anxious".

2 ■ 0

17. **Write down** an expression which shows that the writer did not expect to be handed over as a spy.

2 ■ 0

Think about the whole passage.

18. Explain clearly how the events of this story are likely to add to the writer's feeling that he had committed "a number of idiocies" (Paragraph 1).

2 1 0

[*END OF QUESTION PAPER*]

1995
WEDNESDAY, 3 MAY
1.00 PM – 1.50 PM

ENGLISH STANDARD GRADE

General Level Reading Text

Read carefully the passage. It will help if you read it twice. When you have done so, answer the questions. Use the spaces provided in the Question/Answer booklet.

Timothy, Jane, and their mother, Rose, have found an old cottage with a sign: "FOR RENT OR SALE. APPLY TO BEACH HOUSE, WALLNEY." The children have persuaded Rose—against her better judgement—to enquire about renting it, even though it has stood empty for years.

1 Quarter of a mile up the path, they came to the village of Wallney. Not much of a village: four big farmhouses, a couple of rows of flint-and-brick cottages, pub, sub-post office and an old-fashioned red phone-box. But enough to half-restore Rose's sanity. The owner of the cottage wouldn't want to let it just for a week, or even a fortnight. This was no holiday cottage. The thought brought relief.

2 But there stood Beach House, one of the four farmhouses. Well kept, but not a working farm. Weeds grew in front of the barn doors. Rose walked up the tidy front garden, and knocked on the door of the little glass porch. Too late, she realised the front door was never used. The porch was full of potted plants, several big ones right in front of the door itself.

3 An inner door opened, and a grey-haired woman in spectacles appeared. Respectable-dowdy, with sharp blue eyes and a very stubborn mouth. She gestured angrily, indicating some other entrance that should be used. It put poor Rose one-down from the start. She blundered for a long time round the barns and farmyard, trying to find a way through, until finally the woman opened a door in a six-foot wall, and looked at her as if she was an idiot.

4 "We've come," faltered Rose, "about renting the cottage. Only for a week or a fortnight . . ." She was almost ready to take to her heels and run. Only the small eager figures on each side of her kept her steady.

5 "Oh, come in," said the woman impatiently, and led the way with vigorous but erratic steps, as if she had arthritis but was trying to trample it underfoot by sheer will-power.

6 The kitchen they were led into was uncannily like the one they had just seen in the old cottage, except it was shining and alive. There was a glowing coal fire, which cheered Rose up, even in the middle of July. A grandfather clock ticked soothingly. There was a bundle of knitting in a chair, and a tray laid for tea, with a glass sugar-basin. Various chairs were occupied by various teddy-bears, one wearing full-size spectacles.

7 And straightaway, Rose was under a spell. This indeed was her granny's kitchen come again. She felt very small, but very safe.

8 "Sit down, sit down," said the woman irritably.

9 They sat, careful not to inconvenience the teddy-bears.

10 "We're interested in the cottage, Mrs . . ."

11 "Miss," said the woman decisively, as if that disposed of marriage for good and all. "Miss Yaxley. Were you thinking of renting or buying? Renting is thirty pounds a week; buying is fifteen thousand including the furniture thrown in."

12 Rose gasped at such bluntness.

13 "What's it called?"

14 "Beach Cottage. Belonged to my brother. Just inherited it under his will. *I've* got no use for it. Takes me all my time to keep this place going, at my time of life. Much too much for me. Much too much."

15 "We thought we'd like to try it for a week . . ." said Rose. "To see if the children like it. Then perhaps . . ."

16 She was sure this woman would sweep away her nonsense with a flood of biting common sense. But Miss Yaxley seemed to be very much in two minds. She turned aside, and rubbed at a tiny spot on the chrome teapot, as if it was annoying her intensely.

17 "It's no place for children," she said in a low voice. "My brother was an old man . . ."

18 "I think it's great," said Timothy, turning on his most charming smile like a searchlight. He had a swift eye for adult indecision. But Rose thought for once Timothy had overreached himself. Miss Yaxley gave him a grim look, as if to say children should be seen but not heard. She seemed to come to a decision and Rose was sure the answer would be no.

19 So she was all the more amazed when Miss Yaxley said, "Very well. I don't suppose a week can do any harm." She was still vigorously rubbing away at the spot on the teapot, which showed no sign of moving. Then she said, rather grudgingly but also rather guiltily, "I'll only charge twenty pounds for the first week. You'll have to clean the place up. Men live in *such* a muddle. They're *hopeless*. But I'd like the rent in advance. Weekly in advance."

20 There was more thissing and thatting, but in the end Miss Yaxley drove them back herself in her battered Morris Minor with the dry bird-droppings turning into rust-stains on the bonnet. Rose thought that, having made her mind up, Miss Yaxley was not only keen to get them into the cottage, but also curiously keen to get rid of them.

21 They were done and settled in by nine. The children had truly amazed her. Rose was astonished that children could work so hard. Still, the whole thing *had* been their idea.

22 Timothy, who was practical like his Dad, had discovered a drum of paraffin in a lean-to, filled the oil-lamps and got them going. He used more paraffin, in a careful calculating way that brought her out in a cold sweat, to get the fire in the kitchen range going. He had also got the water-pump over the sink to work. At first it had only made disgusting wheezing sounds, but Tim had poured water down it from a butt in the garden, calling it "priming the pump" very professionally. At first it had pumped evil rusty red stuff, but now it ran clear, though Rose had visions of outbreaks of cholera and typhoid, and hurried dashes to the hospital in Norwich, and how would you ever get an ambulance up that path, but if you boiled all the water . . . Now he was winding up all the clocks and really getting them ticking.

23 And Jane had sweated up the path many times with the luggage and then gone with a huge list of groceries to the sub-post office, and staggered back again, still without complaint, and even thought to buy all available hot-water bottles. And boiled huge black kettles, and shoved all the hotties into the beds, which did seem quite clean, thank God, only awfully dusty and sneeze-making. Now she used the black kettle again to make tea, and settled down to drink hers.

24 "We're a nine-days' wonder in the village," she announced. "Everybody staring at me and yak, yak, yak behind their hands. The woman in the shop asked me how long we were staying, and when I said only a week to start with she said, 'Just as well, my girl, just as well.' What on earth do you think she meant by that?"

Adapted from *Yaxley's Cat* by Robert Westall

[*END OF PASSAGE*]

Marks

QUESTIONS

Write your answers in the spaces provided.

Look at Paragraph 1.

1. **Write down two** pieces of information which show that Wallney was "not much of a village". **2 1 0**

   (i) ______________________________

   (ii) ______________________________

2. How can you tell from this paragraph that Rose did **not** want to rent the cottage?

   ____

   ______________________________ **2 1 0**

Look at Paragraph 2.

3. **Write down two** pieces of information which show that Beach House was "well kept, but not a working farm". **2 1 0**

   (i) Well kept ______________________________

   (ii) Not working ______________________________

4. Explain fully how Rose could tell that "the front door was never used".

   ____

   ______________________________ **2 1 0**

Look at Paragraphs 3 to 5.

5. Miss Yaxley seemed unfriendly. **Write down two** expressions which show this. **2 1 0**

   (i) ______________________________

   (ii) ______________________________

6. Describe, **in your own words, two** ways in which Rose was affected by Miss Yaxley's behaviour.

   ____

   ____

   ______________________________ **2 1 0**

Marks

Look at Paragraphs 6 to 12.

7. The kitchen was "alive". How does the writer develop this idea in the rest of Paragraph 6?

2 1 0

8. Explain fully why Rose felt "very small, but very safe". (Paragraph 7)

2 1 0

Look at Paragraph 15.

9. (*a*) From the way Rose spoke, what can you tell about her feelings?

2 [redacted] 0

(*b*) How does the writer show this?

2 1 0

Look at Paragraphs 16 to 18.

10. (*a*) Explain, **in your own words,** how Rose expected Miss Yaxley to react to her enquiry.

2 1 0

(*b*) How in fact did Miss Yaxley react? Explain as fully as you can.

2 1 0

Marks

11. Describe **two** ways in which Timothy tried to persuade Miss Yaxley to let them rent the cottage. **2 1 0**

(i) ____________________

(ii) ____________________

12. What made Rose think that Timothy had "overreached himself"? Explain **in your own words**.

____

____

____________________ **2 1 0**

Look at Paragraph 19.

13. "I'll only charge twenty pounds for the first week." Why did Miss Yaxley say this

(*a*) "rather grudgingly"? ____________________

____________________ **2 ■ 0**

(*b*) "rather guiltily"? ____________________

____________________ **2 ■ 0**

Look at Paragraph 22.

14. Give **three** pieces of evidence which show that Timothy was "practical like his Dad". **2 1 0**

(i) ____________________

(ii) ____________________

(iii) ____________________

15. **Write down one** expression which shows that Timothy knew what he was doing.

____________________ **2 ■ 0**

Marks

16. Look at the sentence beginning "At first it had pumped evil rusty red stuff . . .". Show how the writer creates an impression of uneasy thoughts rushing through Rose's mind

(*a*) by word choice. ______________________________

______________________________ 2 1 0

(*b*) by sentence structure. ______________________________

______________________________ 2 1 0

Look at Paragraph 23.

17. Write down one word or expression which shows that Jane worked hard.

______________________________ 2 ■ 0

18. Why do you think the writer has used the word "and" so often in the first two sentences of this paragraph?

____

______________________________ 2 1 0

Think about the whole passage.

19. Think carefully of all you learn about Miss Yaxley.

Tick (√) **one** word from the list below which **you** think describes her best, and give a reason for your choice.

excitable		friendly		unusual	
greedy		patient			

____

____

____

______________________________ 2 1 0

Marks

20. The woman in the shop told Jane it was "just as well" they were staying at the cottage for only a week to start with. (Paragraph 24)

From your reading of the whole passage, explain as fully as you can what **you** think she meant by that.

2 1 0

[*END OF QUESTION PAPER*]

1996
TUESDAY, 7 MAY
1.00 PM – 1.50 PM

ENGLISH
STANDARD GRADE
General Level
Reading
Text

Read carefully the passage. It will help if you read it twice. When you have done so, answer the questions. Use the spaces provided in the Question/Answer booklet.

The following article has been adapted from "The Scotsman" newspaper, June 1994.

Washed away

There was a time when almost every Scottish seaside resort had an outdoor swimming-pool, but now there are only a few and their long-term future is threatened. BRIAN PENDREIGH reports

1 TWO seagulls hang in the blue sky overhead. For a moment or two they are motionless beneath the white wisps of cloud. One turns its head and screams something to its mate, some seagull joke about the sanity of those humans in the water perhaps.

2 It is 3pm on Saturday and at this precise moment there are three people in the open-air swimming pool at North Berwick, tiny figures bobbing about in the vast blue expanse of water. There are many more shivering beneath towels around the perimeter. The pool was one of the town's most important tourist attractions. They had galas here, swimming and diving displays that pulled in big crowds.

3 It still has its regulars. Two old women turn up with raincoats over their swimming costumes, so they can get into the pool as quickly as possible. Two old men do synchronised swimming. Others bring the staff sweets or baking. But numbers have been falling for years. Costs are high and the season is short. East Lothian District Council is subsidising the swimmers to the tune of almost £10 a time.

4 Now the council has decided to build a modern indoor pool and close one of Scotland's last remaining open-air pools. It has been there since 1900, an essential part of the North Berwick landscape for generations of holiday-makers.

5 There was a time when almost every seaside resort had an outdoor pool, overflowing with noisy, splashing bodies in the summer months. They were part of Scotland. They are part of our social history. But the bodies have disappeared into leisure pools and onto charter flights to Majorca, and the open-air pools have disappeared in their wake.

6 Anstruther, Arbroath, Buckhaven, Macduff, Prestwick, Saltcoats; they all had their own pools. There must have been dozens of them once. There were separate men's and women's pools at St Andrews, but mixed bathing was widely accepted by the time most pools were built in the Thirties when interest in healthy outdoor activities took off.

7 Portobello Pool opened in 1936 and was considered one of the wonders of the age. It had a diving platform 33 ft above the water, four chutes, four springboards and band music was relayed from Princes Street Gardens. The wave machine was so powerful it soaked the poolside dignitaries on the opening day.

8 The pool became a national attraction and there were 18,000 admissions on a single day, just 4,000 fewer than the number of admissions for the whole of the pool's final summer in 1978. Particularly in the early days, many went merely to spectate or sunbathe, though, unlike some pools, Portobello was heated from the outset, using steam from the adjoining power station. Sean Connery worked as a lifeguard for a while. Now both pool and power station have gone.

Cool customers: there is a breeze sweeping across the pool and the teenagers are shivering violently. But then that is because they are speaking to a journalist and not in the warmed water.

9 North Berwick pool will probably open in 1995 for the last time. Other outdoor pools survive at Stonehaven and Gourock, but neither's long-term future is secure.

10 Stonehaven had 86,000 admissions in 1934, its first year, though three-quarters were spectators. Initially the water was unheated, untreated seawater, changed every few days "as it became dirty". The following year it was filtered, disinfected and heated, and the number of people actually going into the pool almost doubled.

11 In 1990, there were 25,000 admissions. In 1993 there were 14,000. The decline would be worse if it were not for the successful reintroduction of special midnight swimming sessions, which had been abandoned in the Seventies because of drunkenness.

12 At North Berwick attendances have fallen steadily over the past five summers, from 21,177 swimmers in 1989 to 8,154 in 1993. "It will be a great sin if this pool closes. This is character-building stuff in here," says Pat Macaulay, who has swum regularly in the pool since childhood and is here with her new season-ticket and her children Richard and Joanna. Pat Macaulay spent the summers of her youth in and by the pool. It was *the* meeting place, *the* social centre for the young people of the town.

13 There is a drop or two of rain in the air and a breeze sweeping across the exposed location beside the harbour. Is it not rather cold? "The water is fine," says Macaulay. "A lot of it is mind over matter . . . I think the kids are getting a bit soft these days."

14 But there are few adults in evidence at this session. The vast majority are children and teenagers, who form lines by the chute and springboard at the deep end.

15 They complain that the new leisure pools do not have these features, the new pools are smaller and the Royal Commonwealth Pool too far away. They are shivering violently. "That's because we're out here speaking to you," says one. "When you're in it's brilliant." Journalistic integrity demands his claim be put to the test.

16 It is not the cold that hits you, but the mouthful of salt water, as you disappear beneath the surface for the first time. The pool is heated, though not as warm as some indoor pools. But some indoor pools are too warm for strenuous swimming. North Berwick is fine as long as you keep moving. There is something quite pleasant in swimming along on your back listening to the chat of the gulls. It is cold when you get out. The knack is to get dried immediately afterwards and not hang around talking to journalists.

17 Shona MacDonald, the pondmaster, and her assistant Michelle Smith have an enormous affection for North Berwick. "The people love it here," Smith says. "We would buy it ourselves if we had the money."

18 However, East Lothian's director of leisure and tourism, says: "Outdoor pools are very expensive to run and declining in terms of attractiveness."

19 The council is building an indoor pool at Musselburgh and is not reopening the outdoor pool at nearby Port Seton. Work has begun on a £2 million pool beside North Berwick's sports centre with opening scheduled for 1996. It will be open all the year round and is expected to have at least 75,000 admissions annually.

20 The director accepts there is some regret in the town at the decision to close the open-air pool, but adds that there have been no formal protests. "People are just being rather nostalgic. The pool has had its day. It's part of a former era."

21 Within the next few years the area occupied by the open-air pool may be returned to its natural state of rocks and sea. The gulls will have a different landscape to discuss. Only rocks and sea remain forever, but the old landscape will undoubtedly linger in the memory of all those whose guts filled with seawater on a chilly Scottish summer's day.

[*END OF PASSAGE*]

Marks

QUESTIONS

Write your answers in the spaces provided.

Look at Paragraphs 1 to 4.

1. According to the writer, what might the seagulls think of the people in the water?

____ 2 ■ 0

2. In Paragraph 2, the writer tells us that there are only three people in the water. Why do you think he also mentions the exact time, and the day?

____ 2 ■ 0

3. **Write down** an expression which emphasises the size of the open-air pool at North Berwick.

____ 2 ■ 0

4. How can you tell that there are no longer galas at the pool?

____ 2 ■ 0

5. Give **two** reasons why East Lothian District Council decided to close the open-air pool. 2 1 0

(i) ____

(ii) ____

6. The open-air pool has been "an essential part of the North Berwick landscape for generations of holiday-makers".

Write down an expression from earlier in this section which conveys the same idea.

____

____ 2 ■ 0

Look at Paragraphs 5 and 6.

7. "There was a time when almost every seaside resort had an outdoor pool . . ."

Explain how the writer continues this idea in paragraph 6.

____

____ 2 1 0

Marks

8. **In your own words**, explain the reasons given for the disappearance of open-air pools.

______

______

______ 2 1 0

Look at Paragraphs 7 and 8.

9. **Write down three** pieces of information which show why Portobello Pool was considered "one of the wonders of the age". 2 1 0

(i) ______

(ii) ______

(iii) ______

10. **Write down** an expression which shows that Portobello Pool was popular with people from all over the country.

______ 2 ■ 0

Look at Paragraphs 10 and 11.

11. **In your own words**, give **two** reasons why the number of swimmers at Stonehaven Pool increased in 1935. 2 1 0

(i) ______

(ii) ______

12. What was the effect of the "reintroduction of special midnight swimming sessions"?

______

______ 2 1 0

Look at Paragraphs 12 and 13.

13. How do the attendance **figures** given in paragraph 12 show that the writer is closely interested in North Berwick Pool?

______ 2 ■ 0

Marks

14. Pat Macaulay says, "This is character-building stuff in here".
Write down something else she says which continues this idea.

____ 2 ■ 0

15. "It was *the* meeting place, *the* social centre . . ." (Paragraph 12)
The writer uses italics to show that the word "*the*" has a particular meaning here. What do you think that meaning is?

____ 2 ■ 0

Look at Paragraphs 14 to 16.

16. What things do young people dislike about the new leisure pools?

____

____ 2 1 0

17. "When you're in it's brilliant." (Paragraph 15)

(*a*) How does the writer test this claim?

____ 2 ■ 0

(*b*) Explain why he feels the need to test it.

____

____ 2 1 0

18. (*a*) **Write down two** things the writer seems to like about North Berwick Pool. 2 1 0

(i) ____

(ii) ____

(*b*) **Write down two** things he seems to dislike about it. 2 1 0

(i) ____

(ii) ____

Marks

Look at Paragraph 20.

19. "... there is some regret ... at the decision to close the open-air pool"

(a) **Write down** another expression from this paragraph which indicates people's feelings about the closure.

2 ■ 0

(b) Explain **in your own words** what this expression tells you about people's feelings.

2 1 0

Think about the passage as a whole.

20. This article was taken from a newspaper.
Write down any **three** features of it which are typical of a newspaper article.

2 1 0

(i)

(ii)

(iii)

21. Explain how the title relates to the content of the passage.

2 1 0

22. (a) What unusual idea does the writer use at the beginning and ending of the passage?

2 1 0

(b) What effect does this have?

2 ■ 0

[*END OF QUESTION PAPER*]

1997
WEDNESDAY, 7 MAY
1.00 PM – 1.50 PM

ENGLISH
STANDARD GRADE
General Level
Reading
Text

Read carefully the passage. It will help if you read it twice. When you have done so, answer the questions. Use the spaces provided in the Question/Answer booklet.

Tunes For Bears To Dance To

1 Henry had been impatient for the cast to be removed so that he could return to his job as the bender for Mr Hairston at the Corner Market. Mr Hairston had a back problem and found it hard to bend over. Henry did the bending for him. Picked up whatever fell on the floor. Reached for merchandise on the lower shelves to fill the customers' orders. He also had other duties. Helped unload the boxes and crates that arrived from the wholesalers. Stocked the shelves. Bagged the potatoes in the cellar, then carried them upstairs to the produce section. Mr Hairston was proud of his produce. Fresh lettuce and carrots and spinach and such extras as parsnips and mushrooms, all of them in neat display at the rear of the store.

2 Henry worked at the store every day after school and on Saturday mornings. Until, that is, he had broken his kneecap, tripping, then falling down the bottom steps of the house just as school ended in June. A hair-line fracture, the doctor had said, nothing serious, but serious enough for a cast that enclosed his calf and knee. Mr Hairston said he would keep his job open until his knee was healed.

3 "How will you bend over?" Henry had asked.

4 "I won't stock the lower shelves until you come back."

5 "Who'll sweep the floors and put up the potatoes?"

6 Mr Hairston had scowled without answering. He scowled most of the time, his expression as sour as the pickles in the wooden barrel near the cash register.

7 Five weeks later when Henry reported to the store without his crutches, ready for work, Mr Hairston merely grunted.

8 "Potatoes to bag up," he called over the shoulder of a customer, and Henry made his way down to the cellar, where a bin of potatoes awaited him. He always tried to hurry the job because the cellar was dark and damp and he often heard rats scurrying across the floor. One day, a grey rat squirted out of a bag of potatoes and Henry had leapt with fright, his heart exploding in his chest. He was afraid of a lot of things — the closet door that never stayed closed in his bedroom, spooky movies about vampires — but most of all, the rats.

9 When he came back upstairs, Mr Hairston was saying goodbye to a customer Henry recognized as Mrs Pierce, who lived on the first floor of his tenement. Smiling and nodding, Mr Hairston led her to the door and closed it softly after her.

10 "Disgusting, the wart on her chin, hairs growing out of it," he said, returning to the register, a sneer replacing the smile. Actually, his smile was merely a rearrangement of his lips, his usual sneer turned inside out. Henry was amazed at how Mr Hairston treated his customers.

11 "The customer's always right," he proclaimed one day, as if he could read Henry's mind. "But only in the store. When buying. Otherwise, they're only people. Stupid, most of them. Don't even know a bargain when they see one. So, why give them a bargain?"

12 He handed Henry a candy bar, which astounded the boy because Mr Hairston had never before given him a treat. "Eat," he said. Then, "It was nice with the customers during the war, though. Rationing. People came running if they heard I had got butter in. Or cigarettes."

13 Henry listened, his cheeks bulging with the candy while Mr Hairston looked off, as if he were talking to himself, his voice almost dreamy. "I'd make them line up. Make them wait, acting like the stuff hadn't arrived yet but was expected any minute. All the time the order was here and they waited in line. I was like a dictator, the way they treated me. I *was* a dictator. Because I had control over them." Then looking down as if discovering Henry's presence after having forgotten him there, he said, "Go to work. I don't pay you to hang around doing nothing."

14 Just before closing time, while Henry was sweeping the floor, Mr Hairston's daughter came into the store. She appeared at the back door, having descended from the tenement above, where Mr Hairston lived with his wife, whom Henry had never seen, and the girl, whose name was Doris. Doris was a whisper of a girl, slender, with long black curls that reached her shoulders, a bow in her hair. It always looked like the same bow but the colours were different, red and yellow and blue, bright and vivid colours in contrast with her pale, white face, the dark eyes deep in their sockets, like the windows of a haunted house.

15 She usually came and went like a ghost, appearing suddenly and then fading away, a door closing softly behind her or the rustle of her clothing faint in the air. Sometimes he didn't see her at all but sensed her presence somewhere in the store. She was a year ahead of him in school and when they met in the corridor she lowered her eyes and looked away. She always carried library books in her arms. In the store he sometimes felt those haunted eyes upon him, turned and almost saw her, then heard the back door closing softly. They had never spoken a word to each other.

16 Whenever Mr Hairston saw her in the store, he would order her to leave. "Upstairs," he'd command, his hand pointing to the ceiling.

17 That afternoon the girl spoke to Henry for the first time, a brief word, "Hello." So brief and whispered that at first he doubted his ears. She didn't smile at him but her expression changed, or rather an expression of some kind filled the usual blankness of her face. He could not read that expression. As she turned away before he could return her greeting — if it *had* been a greeting — he noticed a bruise on her cheek, purple and ugly.

18 "What happened to your cheek?" he asked, whispering for some reason.

19 "Upstairs!"

20 Mr Hairston's voice was like thunder in the quiet store and Henry leapt with surprise as he turned to confront the store owner, whose face was dark with anger.

21 Henry began to sweep furiously and heard the girl's footsteps fading, the door opening and closing.

22 "She fell down," Mr Hairston said while Henry swept the same spot over and over. "Clumsy girl, always hurting herself."

23 A late customer entered the store and Mr Hairston turned away, cursing beneath his breath. He hated last-minute customers.

24 That night Henry thought of Doris, who was clumsy and fell down a lot and hurt herself. He prayed to keep her safe from harm.

Adapted from *Tunes For Bears To Dance To* by Robert Cormier

[*END OF PASSAGE*]

Marks

QUESTIONS

Write your answers in the spaces provided.

Look at Paragraphs 1 and 2.

1. Why had Henry been "impatient"? 2 1 0

2. Why did Mr Hairston need a "bender"? 2 1 0

3. (*a*) **Write down three** things Henry did as part of his "other duties". 2 1 0

(i)

(ii)

(iii)

(*b*) How does the writer's sentence construction in Paragraph 1 draw attention to the variety of actions Henry has to carry out? 2 1 0

Look at Paragraphs 7 and 8.

4. **In your own words** describe how Mr Hairston first greeted Henry on his return to work. 2 1 0

5. What **three** things did Henry dislike about the cellar? 2 1 0

(i)

(ii)

(iii)

Marks

6. "... a grey rat squirted out of a bag of potatoes ..." (Paragraph 8)

(*a*) What is unusual about the writer's use of the word "squirted" in this sentence?

______________________________ 2 ■ 0

(*b*) Why is it a particularly suitable word to use here?

______________________________ 2 ■ 0

Look at Paragraphs 9 to 11.

7. (*a*) Describe Mr Hairston's **behaviour** and **attitude** towards Mrs Pierce while she was in his shop. 2 1 0

(i) Behaviour ______________________________

____

(ii) Attitude ______________________________

____

(*b*) Explain fully how these changed once she had left. 2 1 0

(i) Behaviour ______________________________

____

(ii) Attitude ______________________________

____

8. **Write down** the **one** word the writer uses which most clearly shows that Mr Hairston's smile was not genuine.

2 ■ 0

9. (*a*) What is unusual about the writer's sentence construction in Paragraph 11?

______________________________ 2 ■ 0

(*b*) What does the writer's use of this construction suggest about Mr Hairston's character?

______________________________ 2 ■ 0

Look at Paragraphs 12 and 13.

10. (*a*) What was Mr Hairston's **real** reason for thinking "it was nice with the customers during the war"?

____ 2 1 0

(*b*) Give an example of his behaviour which supports your answer to (*a*).

____ 2 ■ 0

11. While talking about wartime, Mr Hairston "looked off . . . his voice almost dreamy".

What else did he do which suggests he had been day-dreaming?

____ 2 ■ 0

Look at Paragraphs 14 and 15.

12. (*a*) Doris is described as a "whisper" of a girl.

What do you think the writer means by this?

____ 2 ■ 0

(*b*) In Paragraph 14, what comparison does the writer use to describe her eyes?

____ 2 ■ 0

(*c*) **Write down three** other words or expressions from Paragraph 15 which the writer uses to convey a similar idea about Doris. 2 1 0

(i) ____

(ii) ____

(iii) ____

13. **Write down** the **two separate words** which best convey the contrast between Doris's face and her bows.

[ ] and [ ] 2 ■ 0

14. Give **two** pieces of evidence which suggest that Doris was shy. 2 1 0

(i) ____

(ii) ____

Look at Paragraphs 17 and 18.

15. (*a*) What unusual thing happened that afternoon?

2 1 0

(*b*) Explain **in your own words** why Henry "doubted his ears".

2 1 0

(*c*) **Write down** an expression from later in Paragraph 17 which repeats this idea of doubt.

2 ■ 0

16. When Henry asked Doris about her cheek, he whispered "for some reason". What reason do you think he had for whispering?

2 ■ 0

Look at Paragraphs 20 to 24.

17. Mr Hairston's face was "dark with anger". What other expression is used in this paragraph to show his anger?

2 ■ 0

18. "Henry began to sweep furiously" (Paragraph 21)
". . . Henry swept the same spot over and over" (Paragraph 22)
What do Henry's actions tell you about how he felt?

2 1 0

19. "'She fell down,' Mr Hairston said . . ." (Paragraph 22)
From your reading of the whole passage, do you believe Mr Hairston? Give a reason for your answer.

2 1 0

[*END OF QUESTION PAPER*]

1998
WEDNESDAY, 6 MAY
1.00 PM – 1.50 PM

ENGLISH
STANDARD GRADE
General Level
Reading
Text

Read carefully the passage overleaf. It will help if you read it twice. When you have done so, answer the questions. Use the spaces provided in the Question/Answer booklet.

1998

Why You Don't See Baby Pigeons

1 When I moved to a flat in New York and discovered that my new neighbours included a colony of pigeons, my first reaction was: exterminate the brutes! I cringed at their morning mating calls, and agreed with my wife, Dana, when she cursed them as winged rodents that soil the city. I attacked them with broom and water-pistol. It was hard for me to believe that the traditional symbol of peace, a dove with an olive branch, is actually a white pigeon.

2 Then last December, after scaring away a grey pigeon roosting on the sill of our bathroom window, I found a nest there with an egg in it. "Revenge is ours!" I shouted to Dana, triumphantly holding the egg aloft. "Should I smash it right away or save it for an omelette?"

3 But Dana was looking in horror at the window-sill behind me. The pigeon had swooped back to the empty nest and was beating its wings against the window frame.

4 "You put that back this second!" Dana said, with the same look on her face that I swear the parent pigeon had.

5 "How can a rational human want to save a baby pigeon?" I asked as I returned the egg.

6 And then it came to me. Here was a chance to answer the perennial mystery that puzzled generations of city dwellers: why doesn't anyone ever see a baby pigeon? Let others plumb Loch Ness for its monster or climb the Himalayas in search of the Yeti. I would be the first human to see a baby pigeon in the wild.

7 The bird roosted outside the bathroom for a week, and then one morning the nest was empty—no mother, no baby, no egg. Soon another nest appeared with two eggs, but they, too, vanished.

8 I began keeping a field journal, and named the grey pigeon Medea and her black-and-white speckled partner Don Guano. On March 12 Don Guano strutted about, following Medea in circles around the living-room ledge. Finally he mounted her for a second or two, flapping his wings—for balance, I suppose, unless he was just happy.

9 Two days later an egg appeared, followed shortly by a second. Don Guano and Medea settled into a domestic routine. From late morning until late afternoon he sat on the eggs while she went off. The rest of the time, she roosted while he brought twigs for home-improvement projects.

10 Then, after ten days of roosting, Don Guano and Medea abruptly abandoned the nest. The next day the eggs were gone without a trace.

11 I reported the parenting troubles to Margaret Barker of the Cornell Laboratory of Ornithology. "Eggs normally hatch after 18 days," she said, "but sometimes pigeons are frightened off the nest, and sometimes eggs never hatch because the parents aren't getting the proper diet to make sturdy eggshells."

12 "And why," I asked, "do we never see a baby pigeon?" "They stay in the nest for the first month," Margaret told me, "and grow so rapidly they're nearly full size when they emerge."

13 When Medea returned, I fed her a bowl of cereal mixed with a powdered calcium supplement. I worried about what this was doing to me. Was I becoming one of those people on park benches who feed pigeons?

14 Soon the calcium-enriched Medea laid two more eggs, and this time the roosting proceeded smoothly for the full 18 days. We were ready to make history on Friday, April 21. I armed myself with a new pair of binoculars and a copy of *The Pigeon* by Wendell Mitchell Levi, which I studied with all the care other parents devote to Dr Spock's books.

15 "Wherever civilisation has flourished, there the pigeon has thrived," wrote Levi. Pigeons are found on every continent except Antarctica, inhabiting environments from Alaska to the equatorial islands. They were worshipped in Mesopotamia and sculpted on Egyptian tombs. They carried messages for King Solomon, helped Julius Caesar conquer Gaul and won dozens of medals for combat service during the Second World War.

16 Pigeons, or "rock doves", can fly up to 75 miles per hour and find their way home from more than 1000 miles away. Their primary reference seems to be the position of the sun, which correlates with a pigeon's biological clock. But they can navigate even under overcast skies by sensing the earth's magnetic field. There are "reverse commuter" pigeons, urban pigeons that fly 30 miles a day to fields and grain silos outside the city, then return to roost in town.

17 They are social animals, living in colonies because they gain protection from predators. Poets have praised pigeons' lifelong devotion to their mates. Tennyson linked their iridescent feathers with romance and rebirth in his famous couplet:

In the spring a livelier iris changes on the burnish'd dove;
In the spring a young man's fancy lightly turns to thoughts of love.

18 I quoted those lines to Don Guano and Medea as we waited on that crucial Friday in April. But by evening, neither egg had hatched. I feared the worst. Next day at noon, however, as I watched Don Guano settle in for his shift on the nest, I spotted a bit of golden fuzz moving underneath him.

19 It was a shaggy little creature, lying in a heap along with the eggshell it had just escaped. "Miracle of miracles!" I wrote in my journal. "Yes, New York, there is a baby pigeon." I had never been an animal lover and was not particularly fond of naturalists or the endangered species they were trying to save. So why pigeons?

20 The answer did not occur to me until I visited New York's most glamorous bird, the peregrine falcon, 57 floors above the streets. There was no doubting this bird's power, particularly after seeing the ***pigeon*** feathers in the nest—the remnants of victims captured in mid-air and fed to the falcon chick. But as I looked at the falcons, all I could think was: *You wimps! You wouldn't be here without us! We've spent millions on you; we've banned the DDT that was upsetting your delicate systems; we've built you nest boxes; we've coddled your chicks—all to produce two dozen birds in New York. One pigeon colony achieved that in my courtyard by itself.*

21 A lot of people in the city may identify with the falcon: a ruthless, grandly isolated predator, rewarded with a penthouse view of its dominion. But the falcon doesn't hold the great secret to evolutionary success, at least not for humans.

22 Our species did not prevail over other animals by being brave and cunning solitary hunters. We used our brains to become co-operative and shameless opportunists, able to adapt to any available niche. We may pollute and squabble and crowd together in grimy crannies without views, but at least we're survivors. We may envy their speed and rapacity, but we are not falcons. We are tougher. We, fortunately, are pigeons.

Adapted from a *New York Times* article by John Tierney

[*END OF PASSAGE*]

Marks

QUESTIONS

Write your answers in the spaces provided.

Look at Paragraphs 1 to 5.

1. (*a*) **Write down** an expression from **Paragraph 1** that clearly indicates **the writer's attitude** to pigeons.

   ______________________________ 2 ■ 0

   (*b*) Given his attitude, what **fact** about pigeons did the writer find difficult to understand?

   ____

   ______________________________ 2 ■ 0

2. (*a*) "Should I smash it right away or save it for an omelette?" (Paragraph 2)
   What was Dana's reaction to these suggestions?

   ____

   ______________________________ 2 ■ 0

   (*b*) Why is her reaction surprising?

   ____

   ______________________________ 2 1 0

Look at Paragraph 6.

3. Why does the writer begin **Paragraph 6** with such a short sentence?

   ____

   ____

   ______________________________ 2 ■ 0

4. What expression used later in the same paragraph means almost the same as "perennial mystery"?

   ______________________________ 2 ■ 0

Marks

5. Explain how the writer tries to make the rest of **Paragraph 6** funny.

____

____

________________________ **2 1 0**

Look at Paragraphs 7 to 10.

6. What evidence is there that the writer started to take a closer interest in the pigeons? **2 1 0**

(i) ________________________

(ii) ________________________

(iii) ________________________

7. "he brought twigs for home-improvement projects" (Paragraph 9)

(*a*) Explain exactly what Don Guano was doing.

____

________________________ **2 1 0**

(*b*) To what is Don Guano being compared, and what is the effect of this comparison?

____

________________________ **2 1 0**

Look at Paragraphs 11 to 14.

8. (*a*) Why might pigeon eggs **not** hatch after 18 days? **2 1 0**

(i) ________________________

____

(ii) ________________________

____

(*b*) Why don't we normally see a baby pigeon?

____

________________________ **2 1 0**

Marks

9. What, do you think, was **the writer's attitude** to "those people on park benches who feed pigeons" and how does he reveal it?

____

____

____ **2 1 0**

10. (*a*) **Write down two** things the writer did to ensure that the eggs hatched successfully. **2 1 0**

(i) ____________________________________

(ii) ____________________________________

(*b*) What kind of books do you think Dr Spock wrote?

____

____ **2 1 0**

Look at Paragraphs 15 to 18.

11. "Wherever civilization has flourished, there the pigeon has thrived" (Paragraph 15) What fact proves this statement?

____

____ **2 1 0**

12. What **two** things help pigeons to navigate? **2 1 0**

(i) ____________________________________

(ii) ____________________________________

13. Explain why "reverse commuter" is a good way of describing urban pigeons.

____

____

____ **2 1 0**

Marks

14. Explain **in your own words** why poets have praised pigeons. 2 1 0

Look at Paragraphs 19 to 22.

15. (*a*) Why does the writer call peregrine falcons "wimps"? 2 1 0

(*b*) What **two** things about the way **Paragraph 20** is written show the strength of his feelings? 2 1 0

(i)

(ii)

16. (*a*) **In your own words**, explain why a lot of people might "identify with the falcon". 2 1 0

(*b*) Explain, as clearly as you can, why the writer believes that most human beings are more like pigeons than falcons. 2 1 0

Marks

Think about the passage as a whole.

17. Complete the following sentences to show the changes in the writer's attitude towards pigeons. **2 1 0**

(i) To begin with the writer ______________________________.

(ii) Later he ______________________________.

(iii) Finally he ______________________________.

18. Tick (✓) **one** of the following words and explain why **you** think it is the best one to describe this passage. Give evidence from the passage to support your answer.

informative ☐ surprising ☐ thought-provoking ☐

____

____

______________________________ **2 1 0**

[*END OF QUESTION PAPER*]

1999
FRIDAY, 30 APRIL
1.00 PM – 1.50 PM

ENGLISH
STANDARD GRADE
General Level
Reading
Text

AN IMPORTANT MESSAGE FROM
THE SCOTTISH QUALIFICATIONS AUTHORITY

"Following concerns expressed by schools and individuals regarding the content of the 1999 General Level English paper, it has been decided not to publish it."

NATIONAL QUALIFICATIONS 2000

TUESDAY, 16 MAY
1.00 PM – 1.50 PM

ENGLISH
STANDARD GRADE
General Level
Reading
Text

Read carefully the passage. It will help if you read it twice. When you have done so, answer the questions. Use the spaces provided in the Question/Answer booklet.

The following passage has been adapted from an article in "The Herald".

Just when you thought it was safe to go to North Queensferry

Stephen McGinty faces danger to swim with the sharks

Childhood fears are faced as a shark swims by, close enough to touch.

1 There is a cartoon in the diver's locker room at Deep Sea World. It shows two sharks eyeing up a couple of divers in masks, fins and aqua-lungs. One shark asks the other, "Will we eat them?" The other replies, "No, that thing on their backs gives me wind."

2 As I bent, buckled and squeezed myself into the drysuit, the threat of a dose of marine indigestion seemed a poor defence against the flat-eyed terrors of the deep.

3 I had been assured at the North Queensferry complex that the sharks would have no wish to eat me. I did not look like their natural prey of fish, which are small, wet and flap about. No-one noticed that at the time I felt small, was drenched in sweat and couldn't stop shaking. I didn't feel like a flounder, but given time . . .

4 In the next chamber was the world's largest underwater safari: four and a half million litres of filtered sea water containing dozens of species and hundreds of fish including bass, cod, plaice, bream, mackerel, lesser spotted dogfish, conger eels, skates and sharks. The nine bigger sharks were sand tigers—the largest about nine feet long.

5 All the sand tigers have names like Stella, Bertha, Fred, Barnie and Dino. The largest is called The Preacher because most people see him and start to pray. Barnie sounded like a bundle of laughs in comparison.

6 "Mind, the big one is a bit frisky," said another diver to Stuart Bell, my scuba instructor.

7 "Frisky?" I nervously asked.

8 "Don't worry," Stuart said as he helped zip up my drysuit. To explain, a wet suit gets you wet; the water enters holes in the suit but doesn't exit, so your body-temperature heats the water, providing an insulating

layer. A dry suit seals out the water allowing you to wear tracksuit bottoms and T-shirt underneath for warmth.

9 Once sealed inside our suits, we clambered into a tiny tank, containing only a few crabs, where I hauled on my aqualung and weight belt. Sinking to the bottom I struggled to gain my balance against the backwards pull of the weights and aqualung. Gripping Stuart's arm, I drained the air from the suit and accustomed myself to the sensation of breathing underwater.

10 When I was relaxed, Stuart opened the hatch leading to the main safari tank. Rock walls dropped to the sandy floor 30 feet below.

11 Though the habitat felt natural, it would be impossible to view such a variety of sea-life in Scotland's brackish waters. Brightly coloured fish of greens, blues and greys darted, twisted and turned, and a giant skate flapped over the tunnel as tourists, wide-eyed in wonder, peered up as I looked down into an utterly silent world. The only sound was the rasp of my own breath and the click of swallowing.

12 Stuart descended first and I quickly followed squinting while the pressure built in my ears. Just as on an aeroplane, you can clear them by pinching your nose and blowing. On the bottom I lost balance but was supported by Stuart as I found my feet.

13 Childhood memories of underwater programmes on TV flooded in, mixing with books and magazines on sharks and the film cartoon of *Marine Boy*. Once I had gained some confidence, Stuart returned to the surface to collect underwater photographer Gavin Anderson. It was then I noticed the little four-year-old waving from the tunnel. I started to think: what if I was eaten by a nine-foot shark? Would it scar him for life? Then I put myself in his place. As a small child my only response to a diver being savaged to death by a giant shark just feet in front of me would be . . . COOOOOL!!!

14 Deep Sea World was drawing them in with a blood-curdling exhibition about pirates. Just how much would the business boom if the sharks were to turn savage? It's all very well saying these sharks are environmentally friendly and only eat wee fish. That's boring; it's blood that the public want to see. I inched my head carefully, scanning for Stuart's return.

15 Panic and paranoia rose with my air bubbles as I caught a blurry glimpse of my foe curving around on the other side of the tunnel with a lazy flick of its tail. This sand tiger shark was nine feet long and approaching about six feet in front and above me. My lungs began to pipe the *Jaws* theme up in my throat.

16 A few images from the film looped in my head before it arrived: Robert Shaw desperately kicking at the munching mouth of the great white shark, before disappearing inside; the severed leg dropping to the bottom of the boating pond, a tumbling head, and Roy Schneider up on a sinking flag pole, taking aim and screaming, "Smile, you son of a . . . " BOOM!

17 And then it was before me in direct contrast to the celluloid nightmares of Hollywood. There was no evil eye staring me out, no prowling movement or even any interest. Instead it swam by like a bored fridge. Just then, water began to fill my mask obscuring the view. Once I had cleared it my foe-turned-distant-friend was disappearing into the distance. Suddenly I felt a hand on my shoulder marking Stuart's return with photographer Gavin Anderson.

18 Gavin seemed confident and relaxed. "If we want to get a picture of you with a shark you're going to have to get quite close so I can blast it with the flash and get the shot."

19 "That won't annoy it?" I worried.

20 "What?"

21 "The shark, you won't annoy it?"

22 "It'll be fine," he said, shaking his head and administering a friendly pat.

23 Thirty feet down he fiddled with his camera while occasionally giving the OK signal—thumb and first finger in a circle while the remaining three stick up in the air. I responded, though the mouthpiece hid the manic grins I made.

24 To recap on the sunken scene, I was kneeling on the bottom with my tank to the tunnel. Stuart was stationed protectively to my left side while Gavin hung about on the right, itching to shoot. I felt like bad bait—only crowds of cod, bass and flounder flocked towards me.

25 Ten or twelve of them mobbed round my mask, occasionally touching the glass before fleeing. Then I remembered sharks eat fish and suddenly felt like jam in a swiss roll at a kids' tea party. But they wouldn't leave. Just then Gavin got excited which could mean only one thing— the return of the floating fridge.

26 Earlier, while changing, we had rehearsed how I would tilt my head backwards so that my face and the shark's would fit inside the same picture. But I couldn't do it. I didn't want to. I slightly tilted my head and noticed the soft underbelly breeze above me, close enough to touch. This was real, not an image from a movie.

27 The finest moment of a memorable dive was when we slowly rose to the surface as a giant skate flapped past on one side while a sand tiger shark browsed by below me. The chance of such an encounter in the open seas would be as slim as my chances of survival without Stuart's reassuring presence and training.

28 Breaking the surface and wrenching out the mouthpiece, I swore, and swore, and swore. Swearing is sometimes more descriptive for the indescribable as the words come charged with more impact. I had swum with sharks. Childhood fears and attractions had been relived when I touched another world. I simply wanted to return.

[*END OF PASSAGE*]

QUESTIONS

Write your answers in the spaces provided.

Look at Paragraphs 1 to 3.

1. **Write down** an expression the writer uses which suggests that he was having difficulty getting dressed for diving. 2 0

2. **Write down** an expression he uses to show how he feels about the sharks. 2 0

3. (*a*) What reason was the writer given for believing that the sharks wouldn't want to eat him? 2 0

   (*b*) Explain fully why the writer was not reassured by this reason. 2 1 0

4. "I didn't feel like a flounder, but given time . . ."
   Why do you think the writer **deliberately** chose not to complete this sentence? 2 1 0

Look at Paragraphs 4 and 5.

5. "In the next chamber was the world's largest underwater safari . . ."
   Show how the writer continues this idea throughout Paragraph 4. 2 1 0

6. Explain fully how The Preacher got its name. 2 1 0

Look at Paragraphs 6 to 9.

7. Explain the difference between a wet suit and a dry suit by completing the following sentences. **Use your own words as far as possible.**

(i) A wet suit keeps you warm by ______________________

____

______________________ 2 1 0

(ii) A dry suit keeps you warm by ______________________

____

______________________ 2 1 0

8. Explain clearly why the writer had to struggle to keep his balance at the bottom of the small tank. 2 1 0

____

Look at Paragraphs 10 to 12.

9. Once he was in the main safari tank, the writer noticed various aspects of the fish and their world. Give **three** of them.

(i) ______________________

(ii) ______________________

(iii) ______________________ 2 1 0

10. Apart from the loss of balance, what other problem did the writer experience, and how did he overcome it?

____

______________________ 2 1 0

Look at Paragraphs 13 and 14.

11. Why do you think the writer has chosen the word "flooded" to describe how his memories returned?

____

______________________ 2 1 0

12. The writer notices a little four-year-old watching him.

(*a*) Explain clearly why the writer worried about this at first.

____ 2 1 0

____

(*b*) Why did he change his mind?

____ 2 1 0

____

13. ". . . it's blood that the public want to see." (Paragraph 14)

What evidence does the writer give that savagery is good for business at Deep Sea World?

____ 2 1 0

____

Look at Paragraphs 15 to 22.

14. What effects did the "blurry glimpse" (Paragraph 15) of the shark have on the writer?

____ 2 1 0

____

15. ". . . it swam by like a bored fridge." (Paragraph 17)

Explain how effective you find this comparison.

____ 2 1 0

____

16. **Write down** an expression from this section which shows that the writer's attitude towards the shark had started to change.

____ 2 0

17. Explain clearly what worried the writer about having his picture taken with a shark.

____ 2 1 0

____

Look at Paragraphs 23 to 26.

18. What expression tells us that the writer was still worried even though he responded to the photographer's OK signal?

______________________________ **2 0**

19. **In your own words**, explain clearly why the writer felt "like jam in a swiss roll at a kids' tea party". (Paragraph 25)

____

______________________________ **2 1 0**

Look at Paragraphs 27 and 28.

20. Explain fully why the writer felt that the finest moment was "when we slowly rose to the surface". (Paragraph 27)

____

______________________________ **2 1 0**

21. **In your own words**, explain why the writer thinks that swearing can sometimes be more effective than using ordinary words.

____

______________________________ **2 1 0**

Think about the passage as a whole.

22. "I had swum with sharks." (Paragraph 28)

(*a*) What evidence is there earlier in the article that he had had a childhood interest in sharks?

____

______________________________ **2 1 0**

(*b*) From your reading of the article, how do you think the writer felt about sharks or his experience of swimming with them **compared with his expectations**?

____

______________________________ **2 1 0**

[*END OF QUESTION PAPER*]

NATIONAL QUALIFICATIONS 2000

TUESDAY, 16 MAY
9.00 AM – 10.15 AM

ENGLISH
STANDARD GRADE
Foundation, General and Credit Levels
Writing

Read This First

1 Inside this booklet, there are photographs and words.
Use them to help you when you are thinking about what to write.
Look at all the material and think about all the possibilities.

2 There are 18 assignments altogether for you to choose from.

3 Decide which assignment you are going to attempt.
Choose only **one** and write its number in the margin of your answer book.

4 Pay close attention to what you are asked to write.
Plan what you are going to write.
Read and check your work before you hand it in.
Any changes to your work should be made clearly.

FIRST **Look at the picture opposite.**
It shows the figure of Justice.

NEXT Think about crime and punishment.

WHAT YOU HAVE TO WRITE

1. "It wisnae me!"

Write about a time when you were wrongly accused.

Explain the circumstances and your thoughts and feelings.

OR

2. "Let the punishment fit the crime."

"It's time for a crack down."

"Zero Tolerance."

Should crime be tackled in a more forceful way?

Discuss.

OR

3. Choose **one** of the following titles and **write in any way** about:

Crime Doesn't Pay   The Trial   The Verdict

FIRST **Look at the picture opposite.**

NEXT Think about people and animals.

WHAT YOU HAVE TO WRITE

4. **Describe** a person you know, who is interesting but different.

OR

5. "It's not just a pet."

   Write about an animal which makes you feel this way.

OR

6. "A nation of animal lovers."

   Are we? **Discuss**.

Agree

"Certainly, I would agree that . . ."

Against

"Not everyone however believes . . . "

Persuasive

"Let's look at this together."

Argument

"The arguments really need to be fully explored."

Discuss

Balanced

"You've just got to look at both sides to be fair."

Oppose

"You may disagree but . . ."

Debate

"An explanation is really needed before it would be possible to decide."

For

"All the evidence suggests that . . ."

Question

"Is it possible to consider the point that . . . ?"

FIRST **Look at the page opposite.**
It gives a range of words connected with discussion.

NEXT Think about topics on which people have strong opinions.

WHAT YOU HAVE TO WRITE

7. **Choose one** topic on which you hold strong views.

   Make clear your opinion on your chosen topic, taking some account of the views of others.

FIRST **Look at the pictures opposite.**
They show how photographers from the media can intrude into the lives of other people.

NEXT Think about how the camera can affect people's lives.

WHAT YOU HAVE TO WRITE

8. "From the man in the street to the rich and famous—hasn't everyone the right to a private life?"

Discuss the effect of media "interest" on people's lives.

OR

9. Choose **one** of the photographs opposite and write the story behind the picture.

OR

10. Write about a photograph which has special memories for you.

2000

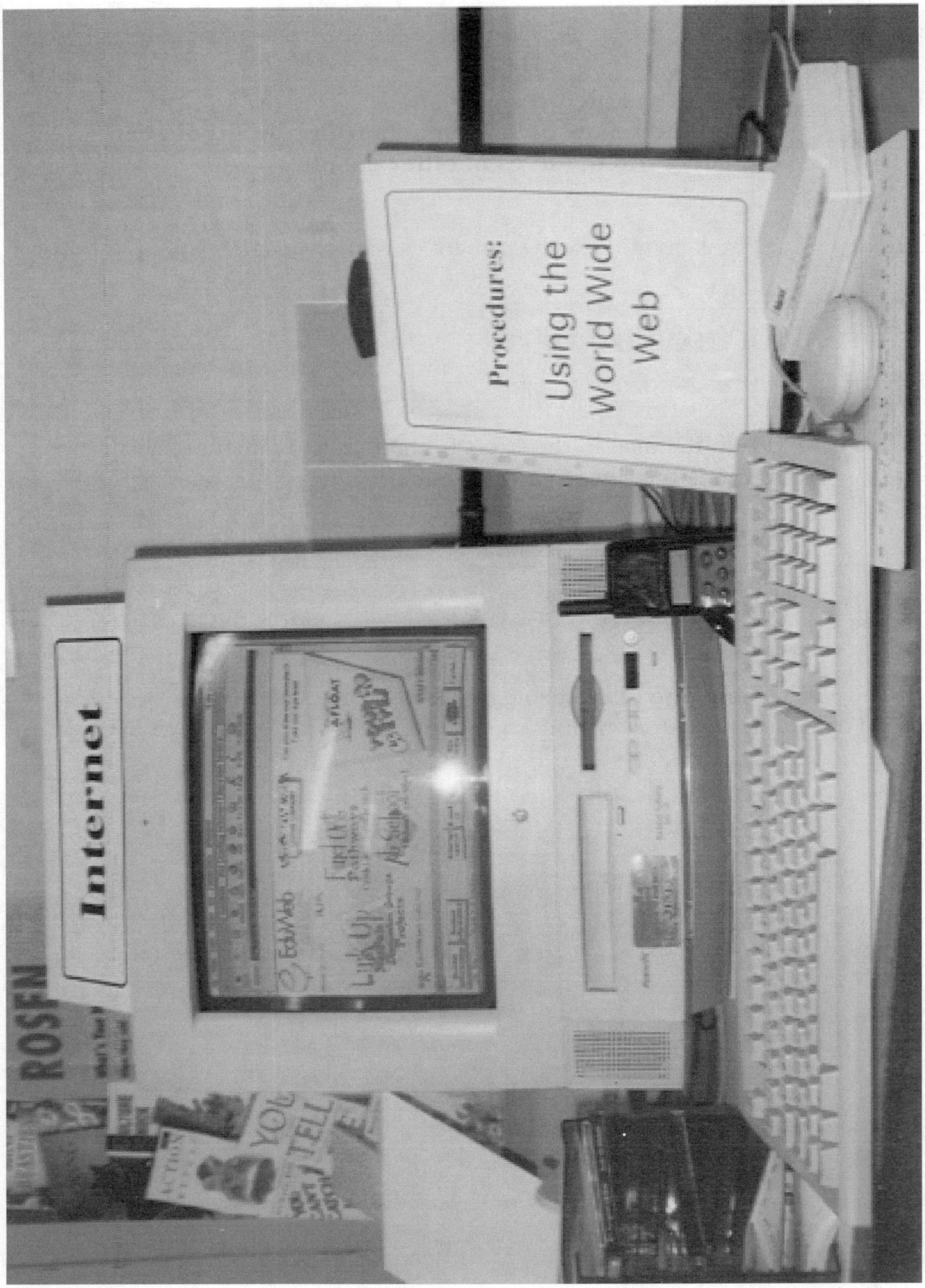

FIRST **Look at the picture opposite.**
It shows both a telephone and computer hardware.

NEXT Think about modern communication and technology.

WHAT YOU HAVE TO WRITE

11. "Computers are fun."

Write about your experience of using computers in your leisure time.

OR

12. Discuss one of these topics:

Modem madness: the dangers of surfing the net.

or

The mobile phone: a blessing or a curse?

OR

13. Write a short story using **one** of the following titles:

The Message I've Got Your Number The Hacker

There are no pictures for these assignments.

14. Choose **one** of the following and **write in any way you wish**:

"Things can only get better."

D:Ream

OR

"Search for the hero inside yourself."

M People

OR

"We are the generation that's got to be heard."

Robbie Williams

OR

15. "Preparation prevents poor performance."
Everyone has to go through interviews.
Explain clearly what you consider to be the important steps in preparation.

OR

16. "Today's parents need to attend parenting classes in order to bring up their children properly."
Do you agree? **Discuss**.

OR

17. **Describe** the scene or person suggested to you by **one** of the following:

" . . . The sun treads the path
among cedars and enormous oaks."

Gillian Clarke

OR

"she sat down
at the scoured table
in the swept kitchen
beside the dresser with its cracked delft."

Liz Lochhead

OR

"Pale rain over the dwindling harbour
And over the sea wet church."

Dylan Thomas

OR

18. You have been asked to choose **five** items to put in a time capsule.
Which five items would you choose and why?

[*END OF QUESTION PAPER*]

Printed by Bell & Bain Ltd., Glasgow, Scotland.